My Buddha Is Pink

Buddhism for the Modern Homosexual

Richard Harrold

MY BUDDHA IS PINK
Buddhism for the Modern Homosexual
Richard Harrold

Text © Richard Harrold, 2019
All rights reserved

Published by
The Sumeru Press Inc.
402-301 Bayrose Drive, Nepean, ON
Canada K2J 5W3

ISBN 978-1-896559-49-0 (softcover)

LIBRARY AND ARCHIVES CANADA CATALOGUING IN PUBLICATION

Title: My Buddha is pink : Buddhism for the modern homosexual / Richard Harrold.
Names: Harrold, Richard, 1958- author.
Identifiers: Canadiana 20190080574 | ISBN 9781896559490 (softcover)
Subjects: LCSH: Buddhist gays. | LCSH: Buddhist gays—Religious life. | LCSH: Sexual minorities—
   Religious life. | LCSH: Homosexuality—Religious aspects—Buddhism.
Classification: LCC BQ5480.G39 H37 2019 | DDC 294.3/4440866—dc23

For more information about The Sumeru Press
visit us at sumeru-books.com

Contents

5   Introduction

Part I   The Basics
11 1 Coming Out and Buddhism
17 2 Are They All Wicked Little Towns?
19 3 It's a lay life
23 4 Four Noble Truths for gays
29 5 Three-Legged Stool
33 6 Five Precepts
41 7 Let's Talk About Sex

Part II   The Noble Eightfold Path
49 8 Right View
55 9 Right Intention
59 10 Right Speech
61 11 Right Action
65 12 Right Livelihood
69 13 Right Effort
73 14 Right Mindfulness
79 15 Right Concentration

Part III   The Layperson's Path to Peace
89 16 Developing a Meditation Practice
101 17 Reaping the Benefits of Your Meditation Practice
107 18 Beyond Breath: Meditations on Body and Death
113 19 Right and Wrong and the Pitfalls of Relativism
123 20 The Elements of Kamma
131 21 Buddhism for the modern homosexual and gender identity variant

143 About the Author

Introduction

Gay people are lucky. All members of the LGBTQ community are lucky, and probably most don't even realize this. We are lucky because while all people are born dissatisfied, we intuitively saw that discord and sought answers. Maybe not always in the right places. But we searched. And in our search, we shattered the oppressive myth of binary thinking.

I know what's on your mind now. Everyone searches for answers. As humans we are innately inquisitive. Regardless of sexuality or identity, we all wish to understand the world and how we fit in that world. But it's not quite the same for gay people.

As soon as we become conscious of ourselves as individuals, we become aware of how we don't fit. And one of the first tools used to coerce us into compliance is religion. Doesn't matter if we come from a church-going family or were raised in a household identified these days as being a "non" – a non-believing family or a religiously unaffiliated household – because the larger society is built upon concepts that originate from predominately monotheistic beliefs.

Straight people do not experience this. The world accommodates them, whereas the world, to us, can appear hostile and rigid, demanding that we become something that we're not. Straight people unconsciously find such a society very comforting. Their very existence is validated by the world around them because they designed it that way. But then we come along.

Our very presence makes many straight people very uncomfortable. In turn, straight society did its best to make our lives uncomfortable as well by trying to force us back into one of two boxes – either we are male or female, and our genitals determine that for us. But we didn't fit well into either box, and that was a threat, so much so that violence became the *de facto* response to our presence.

But it didn't work, did it? Not quite. Some of us acquiesced and lived miserable lives trying to conform to the heterosexual world. Some accepted there was probably some mean-spirited giant puppet-master in the sky that hated us and we had better try to adapt to a heterosexual world as best we could, even if it meant lying not only to our friends and family, but to ourselves.

That was the world I grew up in. Years spent closeted, denying my true self, fearful of being found out. Daily I lived a life that, metaphorically, had me trudging along a stony path from which I gathered rocks that I willingly put into my knapsack. When the knapsack became full, I smiled and produced another bag I would drag along behind me as if I were some unthinking beast of burden, until the load I pulled along was so heavy and restrictive I could hardly move.

All I had to do was let go, leave that burden behind. But I didn't know I had a choice. So, on I trudged.

It is somewhat easier these days for young people to acknowledge and accept their sexuality. This is a wonderful development. But the larger society continues to dictate how we should live our lives; the binary thinking remains. "OK, fine, you're gay, so you're still going to settle down to a nice domestic and monogamous life, right? You got marriage now, no more doing whatever the hell you want. Settle down!"

Even if you're a teen coming out now, the larger society continues to expect us all to follow certain norms. And our choices are very limited. It's very much like the film "Lobster," that depicts a world in which you must be partnered, and if you refuse, you're turned into an animal. If you rebel, you're an outlaw, but even the outlaws limit themselves by remaining celibate. It's all just more rocks we keep dragging around, the only difference being that some of us are dragging granite and others are dragging basalt.

What if we stopped dragging those rocks around? We can. And some of us do. But perils remain, and one in particular is the most dangerous: nihilism. The idea that nothing really matters because we're all going to die anyway is very beguiling. Billionaires continue to build empires with this sort of thinking. As well as sociopaths.

"I'm a good person! I'm not like that!"

Of course you are, and of course you're not.

"But what about the rest of the world? What's the point? I can be a goddamned saint and still the world goes on its shitty way! And when I try to live my life openly, there's always someone who can't deal with it, and sometimes they're really hostile."

I do not disagree. I have felt the same way. In fact, there are times I still feel that way. But it's less often and, perhaps what it is even better, my intentions and focus are keener now, leading me to better results more often.

Following the Buddha's path helped me achieve that. But it didn't happen overnight, and it wasn't necessarily easy. In fact, it remains a struggle. Despite that, I have traveled far enough down the path that I have no desire to go back. Buddhism has reshaped my world view in such a fundamental manner that I couldn't go back because to do so would mean willfully giving up the happiness and what equanimity I have, to return to a much darker period in my life when happiness eluded me.

And happiness eluded me because I, as I learned, was the primary factor getting in my own way preventing me from finding it.

I began by saying we queer folk are luckier than most because we grow up already questioning the world around us in ways that straight people generally do not. Plus, we question and evaluate our *selves* too. We are in many respects skeptical of our own identify. Who *are* we? And what is it about us that makes us who we are? To find that answer, some of us had to destroy our old selves. Some of us had it forced on us when our families rejected us, shunned us, or just looked at us with a bafflement that may have evoked pity within us.

But to be clear, for most of us, we had to re-invent our *selves*. Let me explain with another metaphor: Fire.

Fire most often conjures images of destruction. But there are species that depend on fire for life. In the Great Lakes region, jack pine is such a species that depends on fire to continue its existence. Cones from jack pine are so densely covered with resin the seeds within can remain viable for many years. The trees also hold on to the cones rather than dropping them cyclically as other pine species do.

If a fire doesn't periodically sweep through a stand of jack pine, the trees are overwhelmed by other species and eventually die out. But when a wildfire spreads through the stand, the intense heat burns away the resin from the cones. Afterward, the cones open, the seeds drop out onto the scorched soil, which is now in perfect condition for germination.

Other species depend on this cleansing by fire as well, such as the Kirtland's warbler. This tiny bird depends on stands of jack pine for its livelihood and nearly became extinct when fire suppression techniques of the past wouldn't allow for cleansing fires to sweep through jack pine forests.

Life arises from destruction.

I find Buddhism is particularly well-suited for life situations like this. And while we all face cathartic events in our lives, few actually turn into the proverbial epiphany. Sure, something changes in our life and we may actually alter our course. But something so fundamental as an entirely new world view?

For many gay people, coming out is that moment; it's a time in our lives when we say "Enough! I am tired of trying to be a part of something that doesn't even recognize me. I am through with conforming to a fabricated notion of who I am and who I ought to be."

And so I started a blog called *My Buddha is Pink*, the same as this book. I wrote the blog with hopes that doing so would strengthen my own practice and help me through the next scarifying fire that comes along and shakes my dullness of complacency. I blogged to share the hope I found in the Triple Gem with anyone who cared to take a peek. And now I'm organizing what I created in that blog into this book.

There's no shortage of material out there on Buddhism. And frankly, some of it is pretty weird. But with this text, I do my best to avoid some of the more mystical and magical attributes that are bestowed upon Buddhism and stick to the core teachings attributed to the Buddha. There's no need to believe in rebirth, but if that interests you, there are books and teachers. You don't even need to get a deep knowledge of karma (or kamma, as I spell it here, in the Theravada tradition), but there's plenty on that elsewhere as well. You can believe in no god, many gods, or one god. because none of that has anything to do with Buddhism. And you don't have to be a "special" kind of gay either.

And yes, I do tend to treat this with a heavy dose of humor and irreverence.

It doesn't matter whether you're some blue-haired fem boy who wears sparkle lipstick and dreads the day when you might have to find work that pays a little more than serving tables for all the old haggard trolls like me who smile at your youthful face and ogle your pert butt. It doesn't matter if you're a tired leather daddy who still likes his nights on the circuit filled with slings and handcuffs. Maybe you're transitioning from male to female or female to male, or maybe you identify as male but love dressing as a woman and still having sex with other men. There are no rules about relationships, such as "monogamy is preferred." Open relationships, polyamorous – hell, maybe you don't like sex at all but still identify as queer. Or even straight or bisexual or curious or whatever. Great! It's all good!

The goal is to become a good and decent human being with compassion for others, to do or cause no harm, and find a happiness that stays with you. And who doesn't want that?

Part I

The Basics

1

Coming Out and Buddhism

COMING OUT IS A CRITICAL PROCESS for those of us who identify as not heterosexual (while this community includes gays, lesbians, transgendered people, asexual and non-gender-specific people, I will, for the most part, use the term "gay" as a collective term, using specific terms when appropriate). But often, for many, we slip back into an old trap. Let me explain.

Buddhism presents us with tremendous opportunity at this moment of coming out, but there's a trap if we're not vigilant. Many of us do not follow through on what drove us out of the closet to find spiritual bliss in something like Buddhism. Instead, we wound up again becoming part of something we were desperate to leave behind.

Maitreyabandhu will help me explain this with words from an article of his in the book *Queer Dharma: Voices of Gay Buddhists*, published by the Gay Sunshine Press of San Francisco in 1998.

In his article, "Coming out into Dharma bliss," Maitreyabandhu explains that we in the LGBTQ community feel confined and locked by the various groups around us: family, church, school, friends, work. We feel trapped because while in the closet, we are constantly aware that "I don't fit in, there doesn't seem to be a place for me." In reaction, we become very introspective (sometimes also very depressed!), but through this introspection, we take the first crucial steps to define who we are: we have no choice in this because we recognize society at large will not define us as it will with its hetero children. Consider this passage from Maitreyabandhu's article:

> A true individual is committed to developing self-awareness. Usually we are not very self-aware. We may think that we are individuals, that we think and feel for ourselves, but in fact we are very much determined by the expectations and assumptions of those around us.

We just want people to like us.

Many of us "knew" at some level we were different when we were very small children. In vague ways, we reached out to those in our families for recognition, but our families didn't recognize our out-stretched hands and, as a result, we got ignored. From the beginning, we felt out of place.

As we grew older, sex became extremely important for many of us to replace the affection we missed out on as children. For others among us, we were baffled by all the attention placed on sex. We did not learn about love because there was no one to model love for us, so it was all about sex. But we felt restrained by being in the closet, being hidden from the world; we were hiding from ourselves. Maitreyabandhu continues:

> We can see this very clearly in our experience of coming out. When we come out we realize that we do not fit in the expectations of the group, whether it be the group of our immediate family, the church, our peers or our work colleagues ... In coming out we have to define ourselves as distinct from the group. For me this was a very frightening and isolating experience. I so wanted to fit in. I so wanted to conform to the group. But I couldn't. I was gay. Coming out is a special feat of self-awareness and as such can be the beginning of a truly spiritual life, a life devoted to developing our individual self-awareness.

Those of us who are out can remember the feelings of freedom and bliss we experienced through the simple act of telling people "I am gay." Even when their response was not supportive, knowing we had separated ourselves from these groups that had been confining us was an epiphany that changed our lives. As closeted gays, we eventually came to realize through our own experience that these groups were empty. There was nothing intrinsically part of these groups to give them identity and cohesion: it all came from the outside. We, as gays, saw something else driving our being and that came from within. So we liberated ourselves by coming out and separating ourselves from the emptiness of the groups around us.

But what did most of us do (including myself!) after coming out, after experiencing this epiphany, this spiritual peace? We joined another group! We joined the group called the "gay culture," and some of us, after separating ourselves from the confines of the identity labels the straight world imposed on us, willingly accepted new labels to fit whatever empty personality we decided to adopt: some of us became drag queens, others became leather men, others became the "cute boys next door," others became butch (the moniker "butch" in some variation was the first name I used on the gay chat sites) or fem or flamboyant or reserved – we all had to have our own bars, we had to dress a certain way to identify with our group, we had our signs and labels.

Egads! There was a hanky code!

For trans people, the experience can even be more confining because, as an example, trans men can find themselves among other men in a hidden society of sexism, homophobia, and misogyny that can be truly alarming. The choice is immediately apparent: does one retreat again to the comfort of conformity or make a declaration of self?

After freeing ourselves, many of us willingly trapped ourselves once again.

That's not to say that being a drag queen is a bad thing, or finding that puppy play excites you, or that you're really attracted to bears and not twinky dance boys. All of that is part of our individual identity and exploring the person inside us that for years we were afraid to confront. It was repressed, labeled for being weird, or strange, or "wrong." Particularly if you were someone who had the genitalia of one sex, but inside your were the opposite.

No, having the freedom to explore our identity, a freedom we experienced via stepping out of the closet, is important and vital to our growth. But for some of us, the line between that of legitimate self-exploration and expression and that of unconscious conformity gets blurred.

Maitreyabandhu continues.

> The gay scene seemed to me increasingly characterized by sexual competitiveness, vapid small talk and endless wanting. Its obsession with the body beautiful, with the pursuit of pleasure as an end in itself, with youth and style seemed to trap gay men like myself in either painful superficiality or isolation. The alternative, however, seemed to be an increasingly domesticated 'straight-acting' conventionality.

The very thing, Maitreyabandhu suggests, that freed us, our self-identification as being not with the group and our identification with others like us to find succor and support, can become a trap to ensnare us in the very confinement that we so desperately sought to escape. Identifying with others as gay can be a tremendous positive influence for us, but as Maitreyabandhu goes on to say ...

> We must also be aware of its limitations. In other words, we need to be aware that it is a group, that the gay scene is a collection of groups, all with their accepted ways of behaving, of talking and of acting. If we are not careful, we will move from one set of constricting assumptions to another, our gay liberation will become a gay limitation.

This book is about avoiding that by following the Buddhist path.

The Dhamma is a natural next step after coming out, if we stick with that striving to self-identify as being separate from the emptiness of groups. Unfortunately, most young gays are swept away by the sensual pleasures of the gay scene. I think it comes back to love.

We, in general, do not understand love. Particularly those of us in the older generation. We missed as children the physical affection and affirmation we desired and as a result we missed out on the lessons of love that straight children acquire as they grow older. We tell ourselves, "I want to find a man to love and be with for the rest of my life," but we struggle with this because no one truly taught us about love. We have to find out on our own, and many of us fall into the pits of despair created by the traps of sensuality: alcoholism, drug addiction, and for many of us disease. We become faced with the question "How can I love someone else when I don't even know how to love myself?"

Folks are coming out much younger these days. And what is there to welcome them? Circuit parties, mass consumerism, Ecstasy and sex without commitment. The situation has improved over the recent years, with schools becoming more receptive to gay-straight alliance groups. And many churches are showing more welcoming attitudes toward LGBTQ congregants. But the fact remains: the core of Christian doctrine as applied to the laity is homophobic. And because of that, there will always be within our political system an undercurrent of blatant homophobia – sometimes violent – that will from time to time ascend to dominance.

More always needs to be done – even within the Buddhist community. We gay Buddhists need to reach out and attempt to redirect that wonderful experience we had at the time we came out and show others how to take advantage of that desire to be free of group identification. The Dhamma provides this, and the Dhamma can teach us about love when no one else did. It is a path of peace that we experienced gay Buddhists can document because we have travelled it ourselves.

Coming out liberates us sexually in a very positive way, but remains fraught with dangers as many begin to follow an unfulfilling pattern of meaningless tricks and one-nighters that leave us unsatisfied and lonely. Or, because of our lack of experience with intimacy growing up, we fall into a pattern of superficiality and aloofness of which we are often unaware.

But as gay Buddhists, we can fill that need provided we can show the restraint to resist any sensual temptation; we can show how younger gays can not only love themselves, but others in healthy ways AND open to them a spiritual path that is simple to follow and easily self-verified.

Remember the bliss of coming out? Remember the bliss of finding the

Dhamma? Is there any need for these two blissful experiences to be separated by years of more suffering?

Let's travel the path of peace and love together and discover better ways to engage this world around us.

Final note: Dharmachari Maitreyabandhu was born in 1961 in Warwickshire, England. He was ordained in the Western Buddhist Order in 1990. I believe he is still affiliated with the London Buddhist Centre in the East End, one of the many worldwide centers of the Friends of the Western Buddhist Order, now known as the Triratna Buddhist Community.

2

Are They All Wicked Little Towns?

SOME OF YOU MAY BE SURPRISED that we gays know all about "going forth," but I bet most of you don't realize it.

The Buddha talked a lot about leaving the householder life behind, about "going forth" to follow the path to release. Hence, "going forth" became a euphemism for leaving the lay life and becoming a monastic. The person taking up the robes was "freed" from the constraints and distractions of lay life, despite the fact it often meant taking up a regimented life in the Sangha. There were so many new things to learn, new rules, new expectations, new ways of behaving.

Kind of like coming out of the closet, isn't it? Very similar to leaving all those wicked little towns where we grew up, to find freedom in the larger gay community. But, just as I wrote in Chapter 1, it doesn't take long for our new-found sense of freedom to be overwhelmed by all the games, rituals and shallowness we encounter within the gay community: instead of being a refuge, it turned into another fetter.

Come on, gay people are people, and people play games, create rituals, and many act shallow. It's not just a straight thing. It's a people thing.

That's not to say there is no refuge in the gay community. There's plenty of refuge for us to find. But there are plenty of thickets to ensnare us as well.

The Buddha called these "thickets of view." Having grown up in a rural area, I am familiar with thickets – dense tracts of gnarled trees and shrubs in the woods that are so thick it's really difficult to get through them. The branches claw at you, and you can hardly see through the thick vegetation. In fact, to get through a thicket, you really need to muster all the concentration you can to stay focused on your course, or you'll wind up walking in circles.

For the Buddha, a thicket of views is metaphorical, but with the more specific idea that the thicket is composed of points of view, questions, and ponderings that don't help you and, in fact, confuse you and divert you from your true goal.

In the *Majjhima Nikāya*, a core Buddhist text, the Buddha explains this to a fellow named Vacchagotta:

> Vaccha, the position that 'the cosmos is eternal' is a thicket of views, a wilderness of views, a contortion of views, a writhing of views, a

fetter of views. It is accompanied by suffering, distress, despair, and fever, and it does not lead to disenchantment, dispassion, cessation; to calm, direct knowledge, full Awakening, Unbinding. (MN 72)

The Buddha repeats this for each "thicket" of a view, such as whether the cosmos is finite or the cosmos is infinite, whether the soul and the body are the same or separate, and so on.

Many of us come from "wicked little towns," like those portrayed in the movie *Hedwig and the Angry Inch*. I remember while I was living in West Yellowstone, Montana, someone warned me about the town. "Be careful about this place," he said to me. "It will swallow you up and you'll never get out."

I know when I graduated from high school, which was located near a town with a population of about 800, I couldn't wait to get as far away as I could. As Hedwig sang, *"They're pious, hateful, and devout, you're turning tricks 'til you're turned out, the wind so cold it burns, you're burning out and blowing 'round."*

Ya'll do know about *Hedwig And The Angry Inch*, right? I mean, even Doogie Houser did a recent revival of this show.

Not everyone escapes. Remember Jonah Blechman's character, Arthur Gayle, in the film, *This Boy's Life*? OK, I know this is probably a reference many of my younger readers don't get. But I will make a lot of references to film, more so than books even. And if you don't know a film I reference, take it as a cue, honey, to look it up and watch. Anyway. Despite Arthur's realization that he may spend the rest of his days in Concrete (the town in the film), Arthur helped Leonardo DiCaprio's character, Tobias Wolff, escape.

The thing is many of us create new wicked little towns, and they reside in our heads: *"You're running up and down that hill, you turn it on and off at will, there's nothing here to thrill or bring you down…"*

Often, when I listen to this song, I can picture the Buddha (or maybe Rahula cuz he was such a hottie! More about him later!) singing to me the refrain. *"And if you've got no other choice, you know you can follow my voice, through the dark turns and noise of this wicked little town."*

There's always refuge to be found. And that is one of the key elements of Buddhism, aka The Triple Gem – we can find refuge in Buddhism.

So let's get started with the basics.

3

It's a lay life

When I say "Picasso," what do you see with your mind's eye? I think most of us are familiar enough with Picasso that hearing his name conjures abstract images associated with him, strange and bizarre paintings of distorted torsos and faces. Some of it might even seem a bit creepy to us.

And what about Andy Warhol? What is it with his infatuation with a soup can that he reproduced so many images of it?

While you may have a grasp of what either artist did later in their life, you may not be aware that some of Picasso's and Warhol's earlier work was not so spectacular or "abstract." In fact you might be shocked to see how "normal" some of their earliest drawings and paintings looked.

That's because before either artist could venture out into the world of cubism and abstractedness, into the realm of really outlandish (and beautiful) shit, each learned to master the basics. You can't blow up a person's face on a canvass until you first can realistically reproduce that face as something everyone can quickly recognize.

Buddhism is very much like this. There are some basic elements to the practice that ought to be well-established – not perfected necessarily – as a foundation. For example, there are the three basic elements to a Buddhist practice: there are the Four Noble Truths; there are the Four Right Efforts; there's the Noble Eightfold Path; there are the ...

I know, this is already sounding like going to school when you're given a lot of stuff to memorize and parrot back to your teacher. It sounds like conforming. And if there's one thing about us, conformity is not our best game.

But wasn't it so helpful when you eventually discovered that a fetish is not necessarily synonymous with a kink? Although you can get pretty kinky with a leather fetish. And while there is a color code associated with puppy play, you don't necessarily have to adhere to it. There are some basic tips to being gay that we all learn rather quickly, and not always easily, but once we learn them, we are free to be.

There are basic routines in Buddhism that are best learned early, and learned well, and once they are established, you really can carry on with your own practice that suits your personality and life. Because the goal here is not to become a monk or nun. That's an entirely different and additional set of rules and behavior codes that often get mixed in with Buddhist basics but is, in fact, unnecessary to the lay life.

And that's what we're after, leading a gay lay life (and not necessarily a life of one lay after another).

Developing a routine within your practice is helpful, even if it does seem repetitious, even ritualistic. The Buddha generally didn't have a lot of positive things to say about rites and rituals other than that they can be important and useful tools for developing mindfulness.

That's a word, mindfulness, you've probably already heard a lot about. It gets used rather carelessly by many people. In Buddhism, mindfulness is essential. But while pop gurus might ply mindfulness in $500 seminars to help you be better at school or work or sex or money making, that's not the mindfulness the Buddha talks about. For now, keep in mind that mindfulness means being acutely aware of what is going on around you and what you are doing in the present moment.

Establishing the simplest of routines provides us with structure and discipline. This is important for any practice, whether you are a musician, a doctor, a carpenter, a poet, a singer, or even someone's lover. Heck, even being a good parent, son or daughter, brother or sister, or friend takes practice. And establishing a routine to develop that practice is critical.

It relates in many ways to what the Buddha identified as the Four Right Efforts: developing and nurturing good qualities that we currently do not posses but wish to; developing and nurturing good qualities we already posses to ensure they are sustained; removing negative qualities from our actions; preventing negative qualities we do not have from ever arising.

There, your first Buddhist basic! The Four Right Efforts!

There are other, general items to learn and incorporate into a daily practice. These include learning some basic Dhamma, or what the Buddha taught (I tend to use Pali terms like Dhamma rather than Sanskrit terms like Dharma, I say Kamma instead of Karma, and so on), establishing a daily meditation routine, and learning how to be more skillful in our words, thoughts, and actions – and by skillful we mean acting in a manner that reduces negative outcomes for ourselves and for others.

In short, the core of my "routine" involves daily meditation, some occasional chanting, and some Dhamma reading (which admittedly can get really tedious because of the archaic language and all that blah-blah-blah in the Tipitika, but that's why meditation is necessary, to keep my mind clear so I can think about this ancient stuff and figure out how it applies to today) that is generally about once per week.

I often precede my silent sitting meditation by first chanting three times "Namo tassa bhagavato arahato samma-sambuddhassa," which translates from Pali as, "I wish to revere with body, speech and mind that Lord apportioning Dhamma, that one far from defilements, that One Perfectly Enlightened by himself." I chant this primarily because the sound of my voice reciting the words is soothing, the tone eases my mind and makes it tranquil before I begin focusing on the breath. I also strike a chime bowl as I repeat each line. Again, the sound of the bell fading helps calm my mind.

I do not do any of this because I think it has magical powers, that I am summoning spirits, or that I am trying to make magic on my own. Nor do I recite any of this because I believe there is some deity out there listening to me and is going to grant my wish like some type of cosmic cash machine.

There are some other "rituals" I engage in, but will describe in later chapters.

And by the way, just to clear the air a bit, you do not have to be vegetarian to be Buddhist. No need to give up eating meat. And there's no need to stop drinking alcohol or ingesting other mind-altering substances, nor will you need to give up sex.

But be aware, the longer you practice Buddhism and the more you learn about it, you just might find yourself eating less meat, or even dropping it entirely from your diet. You may eventually give up drinking and all forms of recreational drug use, or you may also find that you just don't imbibe as often as you did in the past. And you might give up sex, but I'm here to tell you that after practicing nearly two decades I haven't given it up and I have no intention of giving it up.

Remember, this is the lay life, how to be an everyday Buddhist and to be as fabulous as possible without harming anyone else.

Buddhism, in part, is about asking questions to determine how things really are. But to see the truth, you have to ask the right questions. And the question on my mind at the moment is whether Honey Boo Boo foreshadowed the decline of civilization.

Homo say what? Honey Boo Boo?

Come to the light, children, there is still hope for you.

4

Four Noble Truths for gays

It doesn't really matter if you're gay or straight when it comes to practicing Buddhism. The basic elements remain the same. What may need some tweaking, however, is how the basic elements are presented. For example, how I explain the Four Noble Truths to a fellow gay would be decidedly different from how I might explain them to someone straight. And the reason I would explain the Four Noble Truths differently is based on my inside knowledge that most gay people don't like to think of themselves as causing their own stress.

"Excuse me? Sorry, but it's the straight world that is giving us grief. I didn't bring this upon myself."

That is perfectly true for many situations. None of us did anything to cause the Pulse shooting, just like none of us did anything that led to the tragedy at the Upstairs Lounge in New Orleans back in 1973. There's no denying the fact that bad shit happens to good people, and that leaves us confused, feeling helpless at times, and even angry.

What I'm really talking about here is the day-to-day dissatisfaction and frustration we experience, that of the mundane. So when explaining a basic Buddhist concept such as the Four Noble Truths to a fellow mo, I do so something like this.

Truth Number 1

Life is dukkha. OK, so I get the fact that this is a strange term, *dukkha*; most of the time it gets translated as something like suffering, or unsatisfactory. Which would mean the Buddha was saying life is suffering, or life is unsatisfactory, but that doesn't quite get it, right? I mean, who wants to practice a religion or philosophy that tells you life sucks? We get that, right? Yet, we have our moments of happiness – times when we're with our friends feeling good, safe and secure. So it doesn't suck all the time.

But that's where the dissatisfaction comes in; the good times don't last. Add to that we get old, so old that the young handsome guys don't pay attention to us any more. So a better way to think about *dukkha* is to think about it meaning *impermanence*. Life is impermanent, as are the good times and people we like to hang with, which is frustrating.

Truth Number 2

There is a cause of dukkha. The Buddha said there are three mental qualities that cause this thing called dukkha: greed, hatred, and delusion, which sounds kind of esoteric and all, but it's actually simpler than that.

Greed is greed, but greed is also hunger, as in hunger for action, hunger for sex. We don't get action, we don't get sex, we feel bummed. We tend to be greedy about material things as well.

Hatred is also anger. We get angry. Don't tell me you don't know any angry queens. We're pissed about how people and the larger society dismiss us. And this leads into the more difficult one, delusion.

Many of us think that an endless chain of tricks is the way we're supposed to live, but is it ever satisfying? Are we ever truly satisfied if all we're doing is searching for the next trick? And the converse is true also: those of us who aren't getting any, who are pining away hoping for true love but never finding it, are unhappy and frustrated and lonely. But are we wanting the right thing?

Which means, if you think about it, all this dissatisfaction is really brought on by us – we do this to ourselves. Yet we think we are these victims. I mean, seriously, you think it's OK to expect people to just say, "Oh, he's gay, so it's OK that he sleeps with as many guys as he wants?" Or maybe you're thinking, "why can't I be as good looking as him?"

Truth Number 3

There is a way to end dukkha. But the only way to really understand that is to be sure of the fact and fully comprehend that we cause our own dissatisfaction. When that happens, it becomes clear: end my endless hunger for action, sex, pretty things, brand new Audis, front row Beyoncé tickets at $500 a pop, a maxed-out credit card – if I stop all that, then I bring an end to all my dissatisfaction. I'll be able to accept life on life's terms. But *how* do I do that?

Truth Number 4

The way to end dukkha is the Buddha's Noble Eightfold Path. Well now, that sounds a bit elitist, doesn't it? The *Noble* Eightfold Path. But if you can get beyond that moniker for the time being, it's really quite simple. Because there are right ways and wrong ways to live, or perhaps even a better way to say it: there are *skillful* ways and *unskillful* ways to live.

The skillful ways bring us what we want – less hassle, more happiness, greater peace of mind and contentment. It's the unskillful things we do that bring us pain, unhappiness, anxiety, fear, and all the other negative feelings we encounter. As we become more skillful in what we think, say and do, we develop a wiser view of the world, increase our skillful habits, and cultivate a wisdom that helps us understand that all things have a beginning, middle and end – not just our lives, but our feelings, our thoughts, and our actions.

Unpleasant things will continue to happen to us because before we got wise and started being more skillful, we were living unskillfully: all our past unskillful actions will continue to bring unforeseen consequences that, provided we live skillfully now, we will be better able to accept and deal with when they arise.

No one is ever converted by this explanation, the reason most often being many people's inability to fully grasp Noble Truth number two – that we are the source of our own suffering.

"What's wrong with wanting to get a front row seat to see Beyoncé, even if it does cost $500?"

Nothing, unless you can't pay the credit card bill when you receive it, because you've been using your credit card to buy a lot of things you want, but don't really need, which has put a huge pinch on your cash flow in terms of paying for the things you do need. And why does it have to be a front row ticket? Is it so you can hear and see Beyoncé better? Or is it so you can tell others you sat in the front row at the Beyoncé concert? Or is it because you want to impress the guy you went to the concert with?

"What's wrong with me having sex with whomever I want when I want?"

Nothing, as long as you are treating your sex partners like human beings rather than objects to meet your personal and selfish desires. As long as both of you (or all of you) clearly understand what is going on. But when you blithely ignore the other's expectations, that he may want a relationship coming out of this encounter and you do not, then problems arise, as in stress, as in *dukkha*.

We think we want real things, that what we desire is real, but when we look at it with a clear mind, it becomes apparent that most of what motivates us really doesn't exist. Bragging rights aren't real; status is not real.

Now let's take a cheekier look at the Four Noble Truths for circuit partying homos and other "sexual deviants." Because Buddhism, after all, can be fun!

Now this – all you go-go boys, bears, twinks, muscle queens, leather daddies, angora queens, closet cases, dragalicious divas, nerds and straight-acting-total-bottoms – is the noble truth of stress: (1) body waxing is stressful, (2) pyramid workouts are stressful, (3) cold sores are stressful, (4) smegma stench is stressful, (5) Christina Aguilera is stressful, (6) a sold-out Scissor Sisters concert when you don't have a ticket is stressful, (7) a Cosmo with too much lime is stressful, (8) new leather chaps are stressful, (9) dance floors so crowded you can't move are stressful, (10) finding out the dude you just hit on is underage is stressful, (11) having your credit card rejected is stressful, (12) not being carded at the door is stressful, (13) learning that you can't buy *The Pool Boy* anymore because Brent Corrigan was only 16 when he made it is stressful, (14) finding out it wasn't just a cold sore is stressful, (15) genital wart removal is stressful, (16) returning home to find out that you already have the shirt you just bought is stressful, (17) finding out your liaison doesn't like to kiss is stressful, (18) worrying that you perspire too much in light clothing is stressful, (19) waiting for your HIV test results is stressful, (20) finding out the Asian guy you brought home is a total top when you presumed he was a total bottom is stressful. In short, the entire glamorous life of being gay is stressful.

And this, my fellow moes, is the origination of stress: (1) desiring a hairless body when your genes come from a gorilla, (2) wanting a chiseled body that that will turn to flab when you retire, (3) needing to look flawless before you go out, (4) not paying attention to body odor before you decide to sniff the swarthy saber, (5) not having better taste in music, (6) waiting too long to buy your ticket, (7) knowing the bartender doesn't know how to make a fucking Cosmo but you order it anyway because you want to be seen with it, (8) not knowing about Bick leather conditioner, (9) wanting to flail about like an unhinged dancing queen, (10) forgetting that interest in you is not always genuine, (11) the fact you're unwilling to live within your means, (12) forgetting that yes we do get old and it will show, (13) you should have bought *The Pool Boy* while it was still available, (14) having a sexual appetite that overrides reason and prudence, (15) see previous clause, (16) you're getting old, (17) expecting a casual sex encounter to be the same as doing someone you really care about, (18) failing to know how to dress, (19) failing to accept the fact that multiple partners means multiple risks and you really ought to get on PrEP, (20) failing to recognize that you just might be racist. This is how you stress yourself.

And this, my brethren, is the noble truth of the cessation of stress: The letting go of the compulsion to be someone other than who you are, understanding that your worth as a person is not defined by how much you spend, nor is it defined by how others view you, and realizing a craving for sex is connected with your self-perceived value as a person (you may be attempting to reproduce the affection you missed as a child), and a failure to pay attention to common fashion magazines like *Details*.

And this, my fellow queens and moes, is the path leading to the ending of all that stress, the Noble Queerfold Path which leads to inner peace and intense orgasm: Right Spending, Right Friends, Right Self-value, Right Sincerity, Right

Honor, Right Compassion, Right Love, and Right Restraint. We will get to the Noble Queerfold Path in Part II.

5

Three-Legged Stool

Riding public transportation in a metropolitan area can be at times – how shall we describe it? – interesting, to say the least. In Chicago, one of my frequent modes of public transportation is the Brown Line. The majority of my rides are exceedingly uninteresting. But there are occasions when even I, my dear reader, have to shake my head in dismay.

One time I boarded the Brown Line at Rockwell on my way to Lakeview. As I was perusing some of the notifications on my iPhone, I became aware of the fresh scent of beer. I looked over to my left and sitting across the aisle from me was a middle-aged man slurping beer from a quart bottle. I glanced at the time and thought to myself, "Well, I guess it's not that bad. He waited until after 11 a.m. to start drinking."

Perhaps my beer-drinking fellow passenger had a poorly developed sense of virtue.

On another Brown Line ride a woman boarded while speaking on her cell phone. A plethora of expletives tumbled out of her mouth with an ease that would shame the feistiest drag queen dealing with a broken heel whilst traipsing through the rain in Uptown. As I eavesdropped on her conversation – she was speaking so loudly it was difficult for anyone in the car to ignore her – I began to learn she was speaking to her son, who apparently didn't want to go back to school (I'm presuming back to college). As she cursed her "encouragement" for him to get off his lazy effing ass and go to school to "make something of himself," I heard her then admonish her son for using the F-word. "How dare you talk like that to me," she said with complete seriousness.

I couldn't help but smile as I thought of the irony that such a fine role model of a mother would be offended by a son who used the F-word. Perhaps she had a poorly developed sense of discernment.

And yet on another Brown Line ride during the holidays after I finished my workout at the gym there was a nut case on the car waxing ineloquently as he admonished his captive audience, ridiculing them for ignoring him and being heartless during this most wonderful time of the year. With a heavy sigh I took my seat and with eyes cast down, pulled out my iPhone to do something, perhaps slip into the gay first jhana (haha, that's a later chapter!) where I find rapture and withdrawal in directing my thought to who's on Grindr at the moment (Update – I am so over Grindr).

He went on and on about how everyone on the car would be enjoying Christmas, opening presents, while some friend of his – who must have been hospitalized – was facing certain death because of the overwhelming lack of generosity of those of us on the train. He even had photographs of alleged friend.

I bit my tongue, because the Buddha instructed that even truth should not be spoken if such truth will likely lead to a – how shall we say? – more uncomfortable situation. I wanted to tell this idiot that not everyone on the train was going to be opening Christmas gifts or was even buying Christmas gifts and that, oh, by the way, we all are going to die, and you know why? Because we were born.

Yes, I'm still afflicted with occasional bitchy Buddhist moments. Nonetheless, I remained silent, thinking about how this kook had a poorly developed mind.

My, aren't I the queen of all that is perfect and good! Because here I am, dealing with my own poorly developed mind, my poorly developed sense of discernment, and my complete lack of virtue.

Well, maybe I don't have a complete lack of virtue, but saying my virtue is poorly developed would be an understatement.

The point is that we face constant distraction in the world around us and everywhere we turn. We see ourselves as we are now, or how we might become, if we lose sight of the three basic goals of Buddhism: the development of virtue, wisdom, and concentration.

Some of us may get overwhelmed by all the lists, rules, verses and discourses within the Buddhist canon and think, "Whoa girlfriend! This is bunching up my panties; I can't deal with all this! I need to de-stress with a cosmo." But as the Buddha suggested to monks who were becoming overwhelmed with the 227 rules in the Pātimokkha (the Buddhist rules of conduct for monastics), everything can be boiled down to three essential trainings.

The Buddha explained it again to a group of Brahmans, saying that if we pay attention to how we act, how we speak, and how we think, we can avoid a lot of problems later on. Evaluating our selves under these three areas is really what Buddhism is all about. The key, however, is to develop our virtue, wisdom and concentration simultaneously so our practice is balanced.

Think of wisdom, virtue, and concentration as being three legs on a stool. To develop concentration (focus in meditation) our mind needs to be free from distraction, which is accomplished by being virtuous. But to be virtuous, we need the wisdom to know what is skillful and unskillful. But to have wisdom, we need to have the concentration to investigate phenomenon to be able to discern how things really are. And on and on.

If we over-emphasize one of the legs of the stool, we will metaphorically fall off our perch, like a barely-legal Boystown newbie who slides off his barstool after trying out his first Long Island Tea at Sidetrack. Focusing too much on one of the three disciplines is akin to making one of the three legs on our metaphorical stool longer than the others. Yet I see many practitioners go running off toward jhana like a dazed queen with her first credit card dashing across Michigan Avenue toward the shrine of Ermenegildo Zenga or Burberry.

Not that I am the epitome of Buddhist practice. I am far from it. But I prefer to think Buddhism is about living rather than thinking. The practice is focused on how we behave rather than what level of self-absorption we think we have achieved and brag to others as if it were a bodhi (awakening) badge of spirituality.

Perhaps the path is like riding the Brown Line in Chicago, filled with opportunities for self-reflection.

6

Five Precepts

OK, THIS CHAPTER IS KIND OF A LONG ONE, but I'll do my best to break it up into sections to make it easier for you to go back and re-read whenever you want. Because we're about to discuss the Five Precepts. These precepts are the basis of Buddhist morality. Yet I cringe when I type that word, "morality," because it's filled with so many connotations, particularly the monotheistic type.

But as I mention in the previous chapter, one of the legs of our foundational stool is virtue – dang, another word that sounds holier than thou! – and the Five Precepts outline what constitutes virtue.

Let's start by listing the precepts. They are:

1. To refrain from killing living creatures
2. To refrain from taking what is not given
3. To refrain from wrongful sexual conduct
4. To refrain from false speech and harmful speech
5. To refrain from indulgence in intoxicants

I know what some of you are thinking. "Wait, this is like the Five Commandments?"

No, dear. The first thing to keep in mind with the Five Precepts is they are decidedly not commandments. These are not absolutes. Please note each begins with "to refrain from ..." Rather than commandments, the Five Precepts are guides providing you direction toward your ultimate goal, which is to be a better person. This book is not the *Michelin Guide to Finding Nibbana* (remember, I said I would use Pali terms, not Sanskrit, which would be Nirvana). It's a guide toward greater happiness achieved through harmless living.

Overheard talk: "So what does it take to be a good person?"

"Well, a good person doesn't do anything harmful, he doesn't say evil or hurtful things to others, he doesn't want to do bad things to others, and he doesn't earn a living by screwing people over."

"Yeah, that's sounds reasonable. I guess that makes me a good person because I don't do any of those things."

DANGER, WILL ROBINSON, DANGER!
MASSIVE DELUSION APPROACHING OVER THE HORIZON!

Ok, so that was a bit melodramatic. Let's dial it back a bit.

"Holy cream cheese cupcakes Batman! That is so delusional that it makes my ridiculously colorful costume look like normal business attire!"

"Yes, I'm afraid you're right, Robin. That is so delusional that it makes our relationship look platonic."

"Oh, Batman, our relationship could never be that way!"

Erm, sorry, got carried away again. Hmm, what would the Buddha say about that? Perhaps something like, "If that were so, carpenter, then a young tender infant lying prone is accomplished in what is wholesome, perfected in what is wholesome, an ascetic invincible attained to the supreme attainment ..."

And that is exactly what the Buddha said, according to the *Samanamandika Sutta* (MN 78).

We all want to be a good person, right? Well, except maybe Boris Badenov. Natasha's no sweet pea either. And besides, they're cartoon characters, not even real. But the rest of us, we want to be good, right? So it's natural for us to want to know what it takes to be a good person.

Many of us reach the same conclusion that my "overheard" conversation reveals. If we do no evil, say no evil, desire no evil and don't make money off evil, then we're square with our kamma and good to go.

This works for many of us homo-hedonists, or so we tend to think. So maybe we do a little Ecstasy at the club while we're dancing. So maybe we like to indulge a little in our porn collection. So maybe we like to cruise the gay sauna from time to time. It's all good, right? Maybe we like to head to the bushes for a little while after the Dunes closes in Douglas, no harm there, right? No one gets hurt, it's all in good fun, and everyone leaves with a grin.

But this is a specious rationalization, which the Buddha quickly points out to a lay follower.

The carpenter Pancakanga, ran into this wandering ascetic with a really long name – OK, I'll tell you his name: It's Uggahamana Samanamandikaputta (and if you can pronounce that, I'll give you a kiss in public, even if you're straight) – who told Pancakanga what he believed were the four qualities that made an "ascetic invincible attained to the supreme attainment." You know, the four qualities I mentioned earlier: do no evil, say no evil, desire no evil and don't make money off evil.

Our friend the carpenter doesn't say anything to the guy with the really long name; he just gets up and politely leaves to go tell the Buddha what he just heard. When Pancakanga tells the Buddha about this, that's when the Buddha replies with what I quoted earlier. The Buddha tells the carpenter that there's no skill in merely avoiding the four things the ascetic with the really long name identifies because a baby can do that. And why can a baby do that? Because a baby hasn't developed a mind yet, a mind that is the source of all our troubles.

Being a truly wholesome person is a lot more complicated, skillful and difficult than merely avoiding bad speech, bad intentions, bad desires and bad employment. Don't get me wrong, as these are great places to start. But if that's all it took, then everybody would be pure and happy. Instead, the Buddha tells us that it requires the skillful application of the Noble Eightfold Path along with relentless execution of the Four Right Efforts.

More on those later.

Think of it this way. Initially, we do good things because it makes us feel better as well as making others feel better. And this is great! But the Buddha tells us we must get beyond that *quid pro quo* manner of thinking and make skillful actions so much a part of our normal daily life that we no longer do things with the anticipation of feeling good about it. We just do it. And that's not very easy. In fact, it's pretty damn difficult.

Then again, that is, perhaps, why they call Buddhism a practice, and practice makes perfect.

So let's cover some basics with each precept.

First Precept: To Refrain From Killing Living Creatures

The First Precept would seem to be the most straight-forward of the five. Do your best to avoid killing living creatures. Ah, but my dears, it's not all that simple. For example, are you following the First Precept when you support a woman's right to abortion? If you like to go fishing and eat your catch, are you following the First Precept? And are you following the First Precept when you eat meat, because even though you may not have killed the cow sitting there on your plate in the form of a deliciously rare rib eye, you know somebody did.

And this raises a very common question to many new to Buddhism: To be a good Buddhist, must I be vegetarian? There are many who will answer this emphatically with, "Yes! You cannot be a Buddhist and eat meat knowing that animal was killed for you to eat." And I'm like, "Whoa, girlfriend, step back and take a breath!"

Remember, the precepts are guidelines for you to walk a path taking you toward becoming a better person. And one of the key attributes you pick up along the way when thinking about this precept is that of being harmless to others, including other living beings.

This is a good time to bring up the concept of Kamma (Karma in Sanskrit). Kamma is actually a very complex Buddhist concept that has many esoteric twists and turns. But for us, those of us who simply want to be better people, it's best to keep Kamma as simple as possible and think of it as representing outcomes – pleasant and unpleasant.

All actions have reactions and all actions have consequences. And often, the reactions we get and the consequences that befall us are not just tied to our own actions, but connected with our intentions behind those actions. And in the Buddhist sense, it's important to remember that thoughts, words, and deeds are all actions.

The Buddha taught that we cannot escape Kamma, it comes whether we want it or not. For example, the fellow who hunts to put food on his table, using all of the animal, and who shares his bounty with others less fortunate will experience very different outcomes to the fellow who spends a lot of money to go on safari in Africa to kill an elephant just so he can say he killed an elephant. And the soldier reluctantly fighting in combat will experience different outcomes from the person who has no respect for life and wouldn't hesitate to kill someone for just looking wrong at them.

I will address Kamma in more detail later in this book, but even then I will keep it simple enough for the lay practitioner whose goal is to be the best human being they can be.

So when it comes to the First Precept, you don't have to become a vegetarian. (Because the Buddha and monastics of old lived a wandering life and relied on others to provide them with food, they humbly accepted and ate any meat dropped into their bowls.) Over time, however, as you develop insight into this precept, you may gradually find that you eat less meat, or you give it up entirely. You may have once enjoyed fishing, such as I did, but then one day give up the activity while still eating fish you get at the market. And you can even believe it morally wrong to get an abortion, but support a woman's right to have one.

Second Precept: To Refrain From Taking What is Not Given

This precept is actually much more straightforward than the first: Don't steal. But this precept also has a connection with the Third Precept regarding sex, which should become apparent when it's addressed in the next section.

Having said that, it would be unskillful to quickly conclude that all you have to do is not steal. Remember that the three primary defilements of the mind are Greed, Hatred, and Delusion. And we can easily delude ourselves into thinking that something we took was not only given, but freely given, when in fact we are so skilled at mental gymnastics that all we did was rationalize getting something we desired or believed we deserved to have.

So, it's important, as simple in appearance as this precept may be, that we contemplate what the Second Precept means from time to time, and that we develop the skill to objectively evaluate our intentions. This can only be accomplished with meditation (remember the three-legged stool?). Following the precepts is one thing, understanding what they mean in your own life is quite another, and developing that understanding leads to wisdom.

Third Precept: To Refrain From Wrongful Sexual Conduct

To say that there continues to be a great deal of disagreement and variation over what following this precept means would be an understatement on par with deadpanning that Imelda Marcos likes shoes. And we're going to get into a lot more detail on this precept in the next chapter, but for now, here are some key points.

For example, the Third Precept does not declare that any of the follow are "wrong" or "immoral":
- Same-sex sex, as in men having sex with men or women having sex with women
- Sex outside of marriage
- Anything outside of monogamy
- Having multiple sex partners
- Any form of anal penetration for pleasure
- Oral sex
- Sex involving kink or a fetish

The Second Precept is actually a very good guide to assist you in determining what is "wrongful sexual conduct." Non-consensual sex, for example, is a "taking" of something that was not freely given. And following that same line, sex with minors violates the Third Precept because not only does it constitute, in most circumstances, a taking of something not freely (read knowingly) given, but most areas have laws that define what is the legal age of consent.

When I first learned of the Third Precept, the words were spoken by an Anglo-American monk at a dhammasala near Lansing, Mich., during a Dhamma talk for the celebration of the Buddha's birth, enlightenment, and death. He laid things out quite simply; that sex is sex, regardless of whether it involves two men, two women, or a man and a woman. Buddhist doctrine does not prohibit sex for lay people. What matters is whether the behavior, and the motive, was skillful.

Skillful? Does that mean only good sex is OK, and bad sex is not? As silly as that may sound, it seemed an odd way to speak about this. Yet, the choice of the word "skillful," I soon learned, was both deliberate and correct. In fact, the precept could be read to say, "To refrain from unskillful sexual conduct." Because use of the English word "wrongful" in most Buddhist references has nothing to do with some moral code.

Sex outside of marriage is moot because in Buddhism, marriage is viewed for what it is, a social contract that is recognized by society at large. There is no Buddhist marriage ceremony or rite. So arrangements outside of traditional monogamy can be managed within the sphere of the Third Precept. But something other than the Second Precept starts to become more influential with these other arrangements: greed or avarice.

Constantly changing sex partners, having multiple partners, and frequently engaging in risky behavior can be unskillful in the Buddhist sense because the activity becomes an end in and of itself. Sex becomes purely mechanical and self-serving, and a person can become superficial in such a manner that even though the sex is consensual, the other person is not being treated as a human, but as an object of desire and a tool for self-pleasure.

We'll cover the nuances of sex within the context of the Third Precept in the next chapter because sex, after all, is a primary way we identify as gay and it's a core part of who we are.

Fourth Precept: To Refrain From False Speech and Harmful Speech

Don't you know we love to throw shade and read people. Doesn't take but one episode of Drag Race to see how highly valued a sharp tongue can be in our community. And for the most part, it's entertaining and seldom truly malicious. We quickly learn to be like ducks and let the words fall off us. But it's important to remember that the Buddha was pretty clear that most of our unskillful actions are with words rather than deeds. It is so important to the path that Right Speech gets its own section in the Noble Eightfold Path (that's in Part Two).

Whether you realize it or not, the Fourth Precept is vital to having a healthy self concept. Ignoring our personal identities would be a violation of the precept. As everyone out of the closet knows, denying our sexual identity is to relegate ourselves to a personal hell. Coming out is freedom, it's liberation, and Buddhism is all about liberation.

Lying is such a major unskillful act that the Buddha made no bones about how bad it is when he was teaching Dhamma to his son, Rahula, who was just eight years old at the time.

... Rahula, when anyone feels no shame in telling a deliberate lie, there is no evil, I tell you, he will not do. Thus, Rahula, you should train yourself, 'I will not tell a deliberate lie even in jest.'

But guess what? Always telling the truth can often be just as problematic. Just because something is the truth doesn't mean it's OK to say it. The truth can cause harm, and the precept covers both lying and harmful speech. We'll learn more about this later.

Fifth Precept: To Refrain From Indulgence in Intoxicants

Yours truly loves his Manhattans before dinner. And I really enjoy wine; in fact I have a small collection of wine. And I'm no stranger to other substances. So while total abstinence is perfectly fine and can be an ultimate goal, anything short of that is not failure.

Remember, it's not whether something is right or wrong, but is your behavior skillful? Having a cocktail before dinner and wine during can be acceptable; even spending the afternoon on the beach drinking mai tais or whatnot is acceptable. It's the over-indulgence that leads us into poor decision-making and messing up our kamma.

The same is true for other recreational substances. Is your occasional use of something interfering with your goal of becoming a better human being? Are you going to try and drive after smoking all that weed? If so, then even that occasional use can be unskillful. If the occasional use doesn't harm you that way, but remains illegal in your territory, that could be another problem causing future harm to not only yourself, but family and friends.

"Gosh, I didn't realize that being a Buddhist meant thinking so much."

Sort of sweetie. Most people don't think at all when they act, they just act. And then they wonder what the hell happened. You don't need to be Buddhist to be able to think before you act, but Buddhism does, in my experience, make it easier to develop the skill to think first before acting.

7

Let's Talk About Sex

Despite the temptation to be puerile, and goodness knows I have the capacity to be as campy as the next person (no promises here either, I might let something slip), the topic of sex is particularly important to LGBTQ practitioners. The issue of right versus wrong sexual behavior – or more specifically skillful versus unskillful – is relevant to all Buddhist practitioners regardless of orientation. But it's particularly important to gay and transgendered Buddhists because for our breeder brethren, sexuality *per se* is not the relevant issue. For us, however, it is.

This discussion has largely been limited to the gay Buddhist community, which presents the danger that it will be perceived by the larger straight community as simply being the queers trying to justify their abnormal behavior. Such a situation is paralleled in the Christian community where Christian gays are put into the rhetorical position of having to defend their sexuality against those who smugly point to biblical passages that unmistakably condemn same-sex activity, while at the same time ignore other passages that have been interpreted to be irrelevant in modern society.

Buddhist texts are just as flawed.

It's not a debate when all one side does is sit back and reply with the childish, "I'm right and you're wrong." Yet the same sophomoric response is frequently encountered by gays in the Buddhist community as well. And there is a supreme irony in all of this that seems to escape many Buddhists, particularly those in positions of authority.

These individuals point to the Tipitaka (the Buddhist holy canon) to justify the position that same-sex activity violates the Third Precept as if they are saying, "See there? It is written!" (although they frequently and misleadingly point to the Vinaya, which specifically addresses behavior in the monastic community, not the lay community).

We come back to the teaching of the Kalamas, when the Buddha said not to rely on something as being true simply because it is written. But somehow, this is ignored because we're talking about the Buddha's teachings here. How convenient that these alleged "scholars" forget that the Buddha didn't write anything down. His teachings were oral. They were written down later, and he wasn't around at the time to provide editing. The Buddha knew that someday, everything he said would be written down, and because not all monks hold Right View (covered in Part Two), some of those transcriptions would be erroneous.

Complicating the matter is culture and its misunderstanding. For example, many Westerners have a perception that Thai society is accepting of homosexuality. This simple view fails to appreciate that just as in American society, there are urban versus rural sensibilities. And what happens and passes as acceptable in Bangkok or Phuket isn't necessarily acceptable in Satun or Phayao.

I also believe that many white Buddhists fail to appreciate the influence Confucianism and Taoism has on East Asian society and thought. Recognizing the fact that homosexuals exist and not harboring any outward ill-will for them does not equate with acceptance. Some of my Chinese friends who live in Asia tell me that they would never out themselves to their parents because the consequences would be swift and severe: the thinking with their parents is, "it's OK that I know gay people, but if my son were gay, I would abandon him in a second!" The pressure on many of these individuals to marry and sire children is tremendous; failure to do so continues to bring shame on the family.

So it should come as no surprise to Anglo-American and European Buddhists that the Dalai Lama hedges in his response to questions about his view on homosexuality, or that many well-known monks from both Theravada or Mahayana traditions tell gays that it's OK, but you should remain celibate because gay sex violates the Third Precept, speaking as if they were Christian Evangelicals who say "love the sinner but hate the sin."

Nor should we be surprised by how the fruits of kamma are brought into this discussion by those who explain being born gay is the result of kamma, with the implication that it was some wrong act in a previous life that caused this.

We ought not be surprised by any of this, but that does not mean that such views are Right View; and in the case of kamma, even if it may be Right View, that does not mean that we ought to view our current condition as a punishment.

So how should we apply the Third Precept to our lives as LGBTQ people? And what did the Buddha say about sexuality?

There are a few points to keep in mind as we think about sexuality, particularly of the homo variety. One point that is critically important to remember is there are a lot of things said under the imprimatur of Buddhism regarding homosexuality, and much of it is complete bullshit.

Now I am by no means a Buddhist scholar, nor have I spent days, weeks and months secluded in a forest monastery in sitting meditation followed by standing meditation followed by walking meditation followed by hours of Pali chanting, all with the energy found in consuming one meal per day. In fact, if you are familiar with the British sitcom *Absolutely Fabulous*, I am probably more like Patsy than Edina. For some, that may immediately disqualify me as having anything meaningful to say. So be it. I, for one, believe that if you want to get funky with the untouchables, you have to be willing to wallow in some shit, because it will be out of that cesspool that the lotus flower arises.

That's not to say that I think the "gay lifestyle" is a cesspool of filth. But let's face it; for many it can be filled with round after round of the same Lady Gaga-esque stories of finding ourselves caught in a bad romance. We either go through the experience of searching for the next disco stick as we show everyone our teeth, or we dream about it, wishing for it, pining for it like we've just channeled Charlene as we go through an existence of self-denial and punishment because we've "never been to me."

Because we've all heard the tired line from the realm of Christiandom of "Love the sinner, hate the sin," – to which I always like to reply, "Darling I love your nails, but I'm just not into that" – it is with an understandably dubious eye that we look at Buddhism. Particularly when it comes to discussing the Third Precept, as this precept is specifically focused on sexuality. For some of us, we may have been attracted in part to Buddhism because it does not come with a blanket condemnation of homosexuality; but as we investigate this topic, we realize that Buddhism gives us no free pass either.

What does the Third Precept say? Unsurprisingly, that depends, as there are a variety of ways the Third Precept is presented. But here are three of the most common versions:

- To refrain from wrongful sexual conduct
- To refrain from sexual misconduct
- To refrain from unskillful sexual conduct

Which one is the correct one? Each has subtle but significant differences. The first implies a moralistic tone, that some sexual conduct is inherently wrong. The second has a similar, but less strident implication, indicating instead that some sexual conduct is improper. But what is misconduct and how is it defined? Is it improper because someone else disapproves of it? If that's the case, I deem all hetero sex as improper!

The third carries no burden, in my view, of morality; rather, it relies on whether conduct is skillful or unskillful. And sweetie, by skillful or unskillful we're not talking about how good you think you are in bed. Rather, skillfulness is tied to what results we experience through our actions (thoughts, words and deeds).

It's probably good to review a short version of the Four Noble Truths for gays: Life sucks, life sucks because we make it suck, if we stop making it suck then life won't suck, the Buddha found a way to live that stops life from sucking.

Granted, life doesn't suck all the time; but when it does, it's either because we made it happen that way, or we are choosing to dwell in its suckiness. If we learn to behave more skillfully, we can reduce those times when it does suck, or for situations we did not directly create, we can face these times more effectively and with a better attitude as well as develop the skills to avoid similar situations arising in the future. In other words, we begin to take a more active role in the pre-production phase of our futures, which is more commonly known as living in the present moment.

And what qualifies in Buddhism as unskillful sexual conduct? Fortunately, there's no reason for us to rely on what somebody else says about it – we can get it straight from the Buddha ourselves. Interestingly enough, the Buddha was surprisingly consistent as well in what he defined as unskillful sexual conduct.

Here's the gist of what the Buddha had to say about sexual conduct: stay away from forced sexual activity (rape is bad); sex with married people or people otherwise connected to another (you're mixing yourself up in their unskillful conduct when you do so); sex with children (I don't need to explain this one do I?); sex with monastics (they have vows you know); or other sexual activity that is illegal (having the law after you sucks).

Now that last one – sexual activity that is illegal – is a sticky one because there are many areas where homosexual acts remain illegal. The Buddha recognized that various cultures have differing attitudes regarding the same or similar activity, and he advised us to defer to local norms. But this suggested deference was not advised because of some immoral nature to the behavior in question, nor was he suggesting that his teachings were dependent on some form of moral relativism; rather, it again focuses on outcomes. Certainly it would not be wise, let alone skillful, for me to cruise for man flesh while in Iran.

And just because an activity may be legal in a particular area does not mean it is automatically a skillful action. For example, it is illegal in the U.S. for an adult to have sex with a 15-year-old, but that same activity is legal in Spain. Does the fact it may be legal in Spain make it skillful? And you thought that I was going to make things really simple for you on this matter of homo sex.

But the fact of the matter is the only thing that is simple is the understanding that sex is sex is sex; it is merely action. It doesn't matter whether it's homo or hetero sex, whether it's group or solo sex, oral or anal, done with costumes or done in a dark alley – it's all just sex.

That's why, regardless of which one you choose to follow, the Third Precept does not say "refrain from homo sex," the precept does not single out a single form of sexual activity. Rather, the precept requires you, me and everyone else to have a clear understanding of why we are doing something – anything – that we understand what outcomes are likely from our actions.

This is a lesson that the Buddha taught a child, his son Rahula. To develop a high level of skillfulness in our actions, we must carefully evaluate our activity before we begin it, while engaged in it, and after we're through, to determine whether continuing with that activity brings harm to self, to others, or to both self and others.

There are many scenarios that we can come up with that present us with gray areas, hypothetical situations that may seem to break down my analysis here, my reasoning. For example, we could compare the skillfulness of two men in Iran who deeply love each other and who commit themselves to each other, both physically and emotionally: is that not what love is all about? Now contrast these two men with a man in Chicago who goes to a bathhouse where he has casual sex with 10 different men, all of it consensual. Which scenario exemplifies keeping the Third Precept?

Not so easy, is it?

My answer is that this is the wrong question to ask. Unless you happen to be one of those men in Iran, or you happen to be the man in Chicago about to enter a bathhouse. The only relevant question is the one regarding the immediate actions you intend on taking, and what results these initial steps will lead to. Are you going to be happy and satisfied despite those outcomes?

The Buddha provided us with five basic circumstances to initially judge our sexual activity, but it doesn't stop there. If we are to act with skill, we must take a closer look at why we wish to engage in sex with someone and what are the likely outcomes for all involved. This means that on occasion, we may conclude that a desired sexual encounter that makes the initial pass based on the five criteria the Buddha gave us is one that we, nevertheless, ought to avoid.

Part II

The Noble Eightfold Path

8

Right View

Let's say I'm shopping – it doesn't matter where, it could be Armani Exchange (though I seldom find anything suitable for me that fits, but I love the ambience! All those Asian hotties that shop there!) or Nordstrom (unfortunately, I am more likely to shop there amongst the straight men who have absolutely no sense of style and who couldn't dress themselves out of a paper bag if it weren't for their girlfriends or wives) – and I find a fantastic pink polo-style knit shirt. The price is right and I want it! But what to wear with a pink polo? Obviously, one must wear either black or dark gray jeans or slacks with a pink polo shirt, because wearing this beautiful pink shirt with blue jeans or bone trousers would simply make me faint. Every gay man knows you don't match a pink shirt with anything but black or gray.

That, my pretties, is a mundane example of right view. To dress sensibly, a man must know ahead of time the appropriate matches for whatever items of clothing he desires. Even a basic understanding of style – such as the color of your belt needs to match the color of your shoes – is necessary as a start. From there, one's "view" of how to match items of clothing continues to develop until one becomes very skillful and has his or her own sense of style and taste. But you gotta start with the basics.

The same goes for your Buddhist practice. Without the "right view" of things, your practice will lack focus and direction. And as you progress, without a solid foundation in Right View, it is easy to stray from the path into ineffective excursions of mental and spiritual fits of masturbation: it may feel good at the time, but you're often left with a mess to clean up. Oops, sorry about that; was that Right Speech?

It may help to think of Right View also as Skillful View, as it becomes your moral compass to help you negotiate your way along the path, as well as through the distractions of the world. Consider the words of Bhikkhu Bodhi from *The Noble Eightfold Path: The Way to the End of Suffering*:

> Right view is the forerunner of the entire path, the guide for all the other factors. It enables us to understand our starting point, our destination, and the successive landmarks to pass as practice advances.

> To attempt to engage in the practice without a foundation of right view is to risk getting lost in the futility of undirected movement.

We don't have to have clear and concise views right at the start, views that can accommodate every circumstance, but we do need to have some sense of what is right and wrong, what is skillful action and what is not. Most of us, I hope, know that you don't date your best friend's ex. To do so leads to all kinds of uncomfortable scenarios and would likely lead to you losing your best friend; you know that ahead of time, so you don't date his ex no matter how hot he is. That's a very basic form of Right View; there are just some things you don't do and you know that.

This basic understanding of what is right and wrong is also known as mundane Right View; it's simply a basic understanding of kamma and how it affects you. Doing stupid things – such as hopping into bed with a stranger after you've had too much to drink – can lead to very unpleasant results. To avoid future unpleasant consequences, we need to pay attention to what is occurring in the present moment: that is mundane Right View.

To help us indentify actions that may get us into future trouble, the Buddha laid out for us the Ten Courses of Wholesome Kamma, which can also be described as the ten shitty things to avoid because when you do them, you screw up your life every time.

These ten guides include everything in the Five Precepts, as well as a bit more specificity: don't kill sentient beings; don't take what doesn't belong to you; don't get carried away with your senses or have sex with the wrong people, which also includes don't get smashed because you'll do stupid things every time; don't lie, but also don't go talking trash about other people, even if you think they deserve to be bitch-slapped, which leads into not holding ill will toward others; stay away from harsh speech because it just makes you look like a troll or a member of Fred Phelps' family; avoid idle chatter, which, oh-my-god, is one of the hardest things for we moes to get a grip on; and don't pine away wanting what somebody else has. Finally, don't get caught up in Wrong View, whether your own or somebody else's.

Those are a lot of "don'ts", but unless you are operating from that base, you aren't going to be getting much out of Buddhism. In fact, you'll likely end up like one of those New Age folks who put a fake smile on their face all the time, or like Michael in *The Boys in the Band*: you'll have a bunch of really nice sweaters, but none of them will be paid for.

As Bhikkhu Bodhi says:

> The law connecting actions with their fruits works on the simple principle that unwholesome actions ripen in suffering, wholesome

actions in happiness. The ripening need not come right away; it need not come in the present life at all. Kamma can operate across the succession of lifetimes; it can even remain dormant for aeons into the future. But whenever we perform a volitional action, the volition leaves its imprint on the mental continuum, where it remains as a stored up potency. When the stored up kamma meets with conditions favorable to its maturation, it awakens from its dormant state and triggers off some effect that brings due compensation for the original action.

Ooops, sorry about all that talk regarding Kamma and future lives. You don't have to believe in rebirth or future lives, or even past lives. However, I'm sure most of you have experienced really big payoffs, either materially or emotionally, when you focused your efforts into positive goals. So it may be easier to think of your "future lives" as being what you're going to be like in five years, or ten years, and so on.

You can have a solid practice, one that leads you to greater happiness within and understanding as well as acceptance of the world around you, by simply developing and honing your mundane Right View. But it's only a start, really, as you will fail to gain true insight into your actions and motives unless you move to the next step, what Bhikkhu Bodhi calls Superior Right View.

> The right view of kamma and its fruits provides a rationale for engaging in wholesome actions and attaining high status within the round of rebirths, but by itself it does not lead to liberation … This superior right view leading to liberation is the understanding of the Four Noble Truths.

Ah yes, the Four Noble Truths; there are four of them. Sticking with mundane Right View works well for dealing with the first Noble Truth – that life is unsatisfactory and always ends with death – but for us to gain insight into the endless cycle of rebirth and death of all phenomena, we need to understand Noble Truths 2, 3 and 4 fully. That means we must fully comprehend and grasp how we create our own suffering and how we contribute to the suffering of others. When we realize that, we are able to do something about it, and that is Superior Right View.

Bhikkhu Bodhi explains that Superior Right View comes in two stages with our understanding of the Four Noble Truths.

The first is called the right view that accords with the truths (*saccanulomika samma ditthi* in Pali); the second, the right view that penetrates the truths (*saccapativedha samma ditthi*). To acquire the right view that accords with the truths requires a clear understanding of their meaning and significance in our lives. Such an understanding arises first by learning the truths and studying them. Subsequently it is deepened by reflecting upon them in the light of experience until one gains a strong conviction as to their veracity.

Let's say that while growing up and hanging out with your pals, you heard some of them talk about this other boy – we'll call him Claude – and all this talk was about how hung Claude is. Claude is alleged to have a ginormous penis, but you've never seen it. There is no reason to doubt your friends; some even say they've seen Claude's organ with their own eyes, so you're pretty confident that it's the truth. However, you still don't know it for a fact.

Then the day comes when you see it for yourself; its hugeness is shocking! But now it is also real – you have directly experienced Claude's member (seeing something is direct experience, so don't get carried away with the analogy, OK?), and any doubt you had prior to this moment is completely erased.

Think back to when you were a young boy just before you reached puberty. There's all this talk around you about sex, what happens to your body and what your body will be capable of doing in a short time. Perhaps you've witnessed some older boys in the act of self-gratification and seen its results, so you know that someday you'll be able to do that as well. But until that day comes – pardon the pun – you don't have a concrete understanding of it as something real. When it does occur, it is such a powerful and joyful experience that is can be dangerously beguiling.

As puerile as that may sound, that's the process of developing the Right View that accords with the Four Noble Truths; it is developing that strong conviction of their veracity by experiencing direct knowledge of how they work in your own life: it's verification.

When you reach this realization, your meditation takes a quantum leap into true, penetrating insight. Prior to this, we think we know how things really are, but after attaining this level of understanding, we begin to experience how things really are.

This is no easy task. I am nowhere near Superior Right View, as I am still working on my Mundane Right View. But progress is observable. If you've been practicing in earnest, take a moment and reflect on how some things you just don't do any more, or you do less of, because you have a deeper understanding of how those activities contribute to your general dissatisfaction with life.

And if you're new to the practice, or have been contemplating its potential benefits, think about the basic wisdom and equanimity you see in those who are practitioners. If this creates a desire to be around them – not because they're cute and you want to bed them – then you've already taken the first step in developing mundane Right View. Because this desire you feel is a reflection of the fact those of us who sincerely practice the Dhamma exude a sense of safety: We are safe to be around, we have no desire to harm you or anyone or anything else.

9

Right Intention

A WOMAN WITH RIGHT VIEW KNOWS that when invited to a wedding – regardless of whether she knows the bride – she should not wear an extravagant and glamorous dress that would distract everyone from the bride. Therefore, she dresses smartly, but simply. She has Right Intention: to demure in the presence of the star of the day so that all eyes are on the bride rather than her.

However, if our lady example was a self-centered, publicity whore of a bitch – someone with Wrong View – her intentions would likely be very different. Rather than choosing to dress smartly, she dresses lavishly, becoming a distraction during the ceremony. Instead of wearing Liz Claiborne, she dons a gown by Adrian. Instead of dressing like Miss Gooch, she dresses like Lady Gaga. She has Wrong Intention.

Intention is the forerunner of all action; everything we say or do begins with a thought that arises from an intention. Consider the following from the *Dhammapada*:

> Phenomena are
> preceded by the heart
> ruled by the heart
> made of the heart.
>
> If you speak or act with a corrupted heart,
> then suffering follows you,
> as the wheel of the cart follows
> the track of the ox that pulls it.
>
> Phenomena are
> preceded by the heart
> ruled by the heart
> made of the heart.
>
> If you speak or act with a calm, bright heart,
> then happiness follows you,

like a shadow that never leaves.

Bhikkhu Bodhi states, in *The Noble Eightfold Path: The Way to End Suffering*, that should we allow Wrong View to prevail, the result is that our actions are motivated by Wrong Intention, and that brings suffering.

> When wrong views prevail, the outcome is wrong intention giving rise to unwholesome actions. Thus one who denies the moral efficacy of action and measures achievement in terms of gain and status will aspire to nothing but gain and status, using whatever means he can to acquire them. When such pursuits become widespread, the result is suffering, the tremendous suffering of individuals, social groups, and nations out to gain wealth, position, and power without regard for consequences. The cause for the endless competition, conflict, injustice, and oppression does not lie outside the mind. These are all just manifestations of intentions, outcroppings of thoughts driven by greed, by hatred, by delusion.

Hmm, sounds a lot like the current state of affairs in the world. But I digress.

It all sounds simple enough: keep good intentions in mind and my actions will be skillful and yield good results, right? So why is there the well-known saying from popular lore that the road to hell is paved with good intentions? Shouldn't our good intentions be leading us along a path to heaven rather than hell?

Thanissaro Bhikkhu addresses this dilemma in the essay, *The Road to Nirvana is Paved With Skillful Intentions*. He identifies three reasons why good intentions occasionally appear to produce unsatisfactory results.

> One is that not all good intentions are especially skillful. Even though they mean well, they can be misguided and inappropriate for the occasion, thus resulting in pain and regret. A second reason is that we often misunderstand the quality of our own intentions. We may mistake a mixed intention for a good one, for instance, and thus get disappointed when it gives mixed results. A third reason is that we easily misread the way intentions yield their results – as when the painful results of a bad intention in the past obscure the results of a good intention in the present, and yet we blame our present intention for the pain.

Both Bhikkhu Bodhi and Thanissaro Bhikkhu emphasize the importance of having Right View as one's base, because as long as we're developing the right view of things, we'll be able to become more skillful with our intentions. That skillfulness is developed through the recognition that our intentions can be classified into three general categories: those arising from greed; those arising from harboring ill will; and those leading to harming others. The Buddha recognized there were three ways to counter each of these unskillful intentions, and that is through renunciation, good will, and harmlessness.

My greedy desire for sex could lead me to arrange a hookup with someone I just met on Grindr, but about whom I know every little. However, because I am developing the right view of things, I am more aware of what is motivating me and the consequences of such diversion, an awareness that comes through a deep understanding of the Four Noble Truths. So I renounce the activity of random hookups with Grindr dudes, which counteracts the unskillful desire. Note that I am not renouncing sex, nor am I really renouncing Grindr; rather, I am renouncing my greedy desire to engage in random sex with someone whom I view as a means to an end, that end being my self-gratification.

Because I am developing Right View, I understand that formerly harboring a desire for Fred Phelps to spontaneously burst into flame is not what would be called a very skillful intention. As much as I might enjoy such an event, harboring ill will distracts my mind and will lead to other unskillful actions that will yield bad results. Instead, I worked at developing good will toward the Rev. Phelps, desiring that he will one day see the truth of his anger and delusion and find peace and equanimity. And when he died, I restrained my reaction, not letting myself become gleefully happy at someone else's death, because after all, death awaits me too.

And when the desire arises in me to retaliate against someone for some perceived harm he or she has done to me, I seek to have the self-awareness to stop myself and develop the presence of mind to not harm another person or creature because I feel that I've been wronged or harmed in some way. After all, I must be aware that sometimes shit happens to me as a consequence not just of my present actions, but potentially a result of some shit that I did long ago. None of us can escape kamma.

As Thanissaro Bhikkhu says:

> We start learning denial at an early age – 'It wasn't my fault' – and then internalize the process, as a way of preserving our self-image, to the point where it becomes our second nature to turn a blind eye to the impact of our mistakes.

This is easily overcome with the awareness that you can't think two opposing thoughts at the same time. And because intention arises from thought first before being turned into action, unwholesome thoughts can be easily eradicated by recognizing them for what they are and thinking the opposite: No, I will not lust after this; no, I will not desire harm to befall this person; no, I will not retaliate against this person.

From there we can cultivate the next level of Right Intention by directing our thoughts to positive directions of what we will do rather than what we will not do: Yes, I will renounce this action or belief; yes, I will seek to have good will toward others and engage in activity that nurtures good will; yes, I will be harmless and encourage others to be harmless, and engage in activity that will benefit others.

I strongly recommend you read Bhikkhu Bodhi's section on Right Intention and how to develop the skills of renunciation, good will, and harmlessness. You can find this at the website Access to Insight (https://www.accesstoinsight.org/).

10

Right Speech

Some years ago, well before my mother died, I had the opportunity to spend a week with her in a small cabin by the shore of Lake Huron. We covered a lot of ground during that week; reconciled many issues. And we did it in a loving and kind way.

Among the topics we covered was my coming out to her. She explained that at the time I told her I was gay, she was ready to hear and accept that. But, she added that, if I had told her while I was still in high school, her reaction would not have been welcoming. In fact, she admitted that had I done it then, her reaction would have been ugly.

Most of us were taught since childhood that telling the truth is always the right course of action. But as we grew older, speaking the truth, we learned, was a complicated matter. Our culture attempted to simplify this with colloquialisms like, "If you can't say anything nice, it's better to say nothing at all."

Trouble is for most of us, we are incapable of remaining silent when silence is called for. The Buddha recognized this, and his teachings on Right Speech reflect that while it is important we speak only truth, knowing when to do that is equally important. A relevant case can be found in the *Abhayarajakumara Sutta* (MN 58), which can be read in its entirety at Access to Insight, but which I will summarize here.

Prince Abhaya was goaded by Nigantha Nataputta to test the Buddha by asking whether one should always speak the truth, even if the truth would piss someone off (think Buddha's ambitious cousin, Devadatta). But when Prince Abhaya asked, the Buddha replied that things aren't that simple. The Buddha then replied with guidelines about what constitutes Right Speech. There are three elements: (1) whether the speech is true; (2) whether the speech is beneficial; and (3) whether the speech is pleasing to others.

Thanissaro Bhikkhu presents an excellent introduction to this sutta, noting that the Buddha is not only explaining Right Speech, but he is demonstrating Right Speech in action. Throughout his explanation, the Buddha engages Prince Abhaya, allowing him to present his own thoughts and thus save face through the process.

Clearly, something that is untrue, that provides no benefit and which would just annoy people qualifies as wrong speech and ought to go unsaid. And if something is untrue, provides no benefit, yet would be welcomed by others, you still don't say it. But, even if something is true, if saying it provides no benefit and would just annoy others, it also should be left unsaid.

"Do these jeans make my ass look fat?" "Why don't you try on a different pair just to compare looks?"

What if the speech is true, is beneficial, but would still likely piss someone off? In those cases, the Buddha said it's important to have good timing. That is even true when all three criteria are met: the speech is truthful, provides benefit, and would be welcomed. Even in that case, the Buddha said it is not spoken until the right moment arises. To know when the right moment occurs, we must cultivate compassion for others.

This isn't always easy, especially when we talk of things like coming out. When we come out, that's an example of something being true, that ultimately is beneficial, but which can bring about unpleasant results. We may deeply hurt someone when we come out, but we still do it. The trick is to have compassion for others.

Sometimes when we come out in these circumstances, we are doing it solely for ourselves because we just can't live the lie any longer. If we are compassionate when we do this, we recognize that whomever we are speaking to – a parent, other relative – may be guided by delusive thinking. We may never change that. We can, however, keep control over our own ego and retain our sense of compassion for the other person, even if he or she tells us to get the hell out of their life.

I was fortunate when I told my mother. Although I didn't know it at the time, she already had several experiences that had prepared her for my announcement (not the least of which was that her parish priest was a flaming queen!). At first, I think it did cause her some discomfort. But the timing was right nonetheless. And we moved on.

11

Right Action

THE NICE THING ABOUT THE EIGHTFOLD PATH is that it helps us understand the nature of our actions better, as well as shows us how our actions are connected to immediate and future consequences. Another thing to keep in mind with each of the factors of the Eightfold Path is that they are dependent on each other. In other words, you cannot develop Right Intention without first having established Right View. And developing Right Speech can't happen until you've developed Right Intention. Once we've established a sense of Right Speech, we're ready to work on Right Action, because after all, speech is a form of action.

So what is Right Action? Let's first get out of the way what it is not.

"No, no, don't do it that way, do it like this, yes, like that, oh yes! That's the right action! Woo-hoo!"

Erm, that's not what we mean.

"Well, yeah, he's cute. But he's got all that hair crawling up out of his shirt and up his neck. I don't need that kind of action."

Uh, no, that's not it either.

Let's start first with what the Buddha said about Right Action in the *Maha-cattarisaka Sutta* (MN 117).

> Of those, right view is the forerunner. And how is right view the forerunner? One discerns wrong action as wrong action, and right action as right action. And what is wrong action? Killing, taking what is not given, illicit sex. This is wrong action.
>
> And what is right action? Right action, I tell you, is of two sorts: There is right action with effluents, siding with merit, resulting in the acquisitions [of becoming]; and there is noble right action, without effluents, transcendent, a factor of the path.
>
> And what is the right action that has effluents, sides with merit, and results in acquisitions? Abstaining from killing, from taking what is not given, and from illicit sex. This is the right action that has effluents, sides with merit, and results in acquisitions.

> And what is the right action that is without effluents, transcendent, a factor of the path? The abstaining, desisting, abstinence, avoidance of the three forms of bodily misconduct of one developing the noble path whose mind is noble, whose mind is without effluents, who is fully possessed of the noble path. This is the right action that is without effluents, transcendent, a factor of the path.
>
> One tries to abandon wrong action and to enter into right action: This is one's right effort. One is mindful to abandon wrong action and to enter and remain in right action: This is one's right mindfulness. Thus these three qualities – right view, right effort, and right mindfulness – run and circle around right action.

Yeah I know. That was some pretty heavy stuff. Let's simplify it.

The Buddha is telling us that there are two categories of Right Action. The first one he identifies as being "with effluents." This is just what could be called mundane Right Action because it's tied to everyday activities in normal lay life (Um, and that doesn't mean the life of getting laid). It's connected to the effluents because all this type of Right Action assures us is that we are good people who can expect a reasonably happy and productive life, as well as a peaceful and easy death. In our next life, we can expect to be reborn into a pleasant existence.

Sorry for the mention of rebirth. Remember, it's totally unnecessary to believe in rebirth. All this stuff still works even if you don't believe in rebirth.

The Right Action that is "without effluents" includes those actions associated with someone who is actively seeking liberation, actively seeking release: in other words, someone who wishes to attain Nibbana and end the cycle of rebirth. This more than likely would include monks and nuns.

For most of us, the mundane Right Action applies, which is fine. Mundane Right Action is not lame or unimportant. It's very important. It's just that most of us do not live a monastic life or have any desire to do so.

The Buddha then identifies three key factors that describe what mundane right action includes, and what he identifies is three of the Five Precepts. Don't kill, don't steal, and don't be a whore dog. Just in case you're not clear what "illicit sex" or the Third Precept means for us, you might want to go back and re-read Chapters Six and Seven.

The Buddha then talks about developing the proper frame of mind necessary to abandon wrong action and replace it with Right Action. Part of this includes Right Effort and Right Mindfulness, which, ironically come later in the Noble Eightfold Path. This might appear to contradict what I said earlier about how each step on the path is dependent on the preceding steps. But it doesn't really, because the development of Right Action is accurately described as being a prerequisite to Right Effort and Right Mindfulness. If you don't know what constitutes Right Action, how will you know what the Right Efforts are needed to develop it? And if you haven't developed Right Action, how will your mind be at ease so you can develop Right Concentration?

Look at it this way. If your meditation is a struggle because you're worried about who you slept with the previous night and what might happen with that trick, then you haven't developed Right Action. And if you're withholding your HIV status from your sexual partners, then you haven't developed Right Action either. And all of these examples can be traced back to a failure to establish Right Intention and Right View.

Once we develop a clear idea of what Right Action is, we start to practice it and evaluate our outcomes. We develop skillfulness by paying attention to what happened before, during and after a particular action. What was our intention as a situation developed? Did our action in that situation result with pleasant consequences for ourselves and for the others involved? Will how the relevant situation was resolved lead to more pleasant consequences in the future, or might it lead to an unpleasant situation?

That's a lot of thinking. But it's precisely a lack of this type of thinking to which we can always trace our mistakes. If something went wrong with a situation, or the results we expected didn't happen, it's because we didn't think about these factors or we lacked the proper frame of mind – we lacked Right View and Right Intention. So when you want to get the right action, you need to employ Right Action.

12

Right Livelihood

So maybe you're in a gay club admiring the twinky go-go boy gyrating on the bar and you're just about to stuff a fiver into the guy's AussieBums when suddenly your mind is penetrated with a keen thought: Is this Right Livelihood?

OK, so maybe you're not thinking that. Maybe you're focused on the likelihood you'll get a chance to brush your hand against the supreme package and maybe even get a kiss out of it. Forget it, he's got a boyfriend already. His kiss means nothing.

But what is Right Livelihood? Just some more oppressive rules to restrict us homos into a box of moralistic confinement? I mean sheesh, look what a lot of them try to do to us with the Third Precept!

Susan Elbaum Jootla at Access to Insight writes that our serious consideration of what Right Livelihood means and how it applies to us is a natural step to take after one has been meditating for a while. It is so natural, in fact, that our own growing doubts about what we do to earn money may begin to bubble up in our minds as we become more aware of how our lives are interconnected with social fabrications that continually bind us in the state of samsara.

"OK, whoa dude! WTF are you talking about? Does this mean my job as a clerk in a sex toy shop doesn't qualify as this Right Livelihood thing?"

You may laugh, my fellow queerlings, at my simplistic example, but consider this. Suppose you work for an online company that caters to the gay community. This company's website is filled with important information for the community about politics, social issues and self-help. And suppose it is also a site that actively seeks advertiser money from companies that sell sex toys, pornography and glorify, as well as promote, large circuit party activities that play upon the notion of free and easy sex. Or perhaps it takes money from clubs and bars whose primary source of revenue is through the sale of alcohol. All you do is edit content, or maybe you work in the billing department. The lines are blurred now, aren't they?

It's probably wise to start at the beginning – what did the Buddha say? And in the *Anguttara Nikāya*, there is a very short passage in the *Book of Fives* known as the *Vanijja Sutta*:

> Monks, a lay follower should not engage in five types of business. Which five? Business in weapons, business in human beings, business in meat, business in intoxicants, and business in poison.
>
> These are the five types of business that a lay follower should not engage in.

What does this mean? Jootla explains that the activities "prohibited" to lay followers include "those in which the disciple would be directly, on his own responsibility, involved in breaking one or more of the Five Precepts, which are the very basic moral rules for the Buddhist layman."

That appears simple enough, but Jootla goes on to inject a bit of specific morality into her explanation that may strike one as being absolutist. For example, does this statement go too far?

> Breeding animals for slaughter as meat or for other uses that may be made of the carcasses is not allowed because this obviously implies breaking the First Precept: I shall abstain from killing. Similarly, anyone trying to follow the teachings of the Buddha should avoid hunting and fishing, nor can he be an exterminator of animals.

And what about when Jootla says, "to help others directly in breaking any of (the precepts) is certainly wrong livelihood"?

Well now, what of the earlier example of our modest gay boy who is an accountant with our fictitious website? He's not directly involved in assisting others in breaking the precepts, but he also knows that if the website is not successful selling ads, and if the advertisers believe that visitors to the site aren't clicking on those ads for their products or services, then revenue dries up and our modest gay boy might be laid off, and that's not the good kind of being laid.

In general, we must acknowledge the world we live in and do our best to emulate the practice. Absolutist positions are seldom helpful. We might have been deeply involved in our careers before we began practicing Dhamma. And through our practice, doubts may begin to arise within us regarding our profession and our career path. If we begin to feel troubled about what we do to earn our living and other options are available, then we ought to pursue them. But that isn't necessarily something that all of us can easily or readily do.

As Jootla writes, "… we have to keep a balanced perspective and not keep running after the perfect work – part of the dukkha of the householder's life is the necessity to function in an immoral society while keeping one's own mind clear."

To see how confusing this can get, let's take a look at a Dhamma excerpt regarding Right Livelihood from the *Samyutta Nikāya* describing the Buddha's response to a warrior's questions about the correctness of killing in battle.

A fellow named Yodhajiva says to the Buddha that he's heard when a warrior is cut down and dies in battle, he is reborn in a heaven filled with godlike entities who also died in battle. Is that true, Yodhajiva asks?

It's an interesting passage because it shows the Buddha getting annoyed by someone asking what he calls unnecessary questions. In his reply, the Buddha said that a soldier's mind becomes defiled during battle, filled with ideas that his enemies must die and are unworthy of life. And anyone who thinks he's going to be rewarded for being consumed with such violent hatred is going to be reborn in a realm filled with demi-gods is full of crap.

The Buddha's reply also shows how military leaders have corrupted the Dhamma by tricking soldiers, who knew killing others was wrong, into believing if they were fighting righteously for the right cause, there would be no negative karmic consequences.

The Buddha called bullishit on that bullshit.

It would seem that soldiers and even police officers are not off the hook. This, of course, is clouded by some Mahayana teachings that suggest that warriors can "kill with compassion," but this passage raises serious doubts about such a perspective. Does it mean if you are already a solider or police officer that you should abandon immediately your avocation?

It's not that simple. Soldiers and police officers can and do provide very important non-violent service to the community. But it's important to remember that unskillful acts bring about unpleasant consequences. Think of the battle veterans you may know who suffer enormously both spiritually and emotionally because of what they've seen and done in battle. Or the trauma and depression experienced by many (but not all) police officers who have killed someone in the line of duty.

Clearly, no action is without consequence.

But let's go in the other direction. The Buddha has said acting is a form of intoxication. What do we take away from that? Richard Gere certainly hasn't given up acting since becoming a follower of Tibetan Buddhism, and Tina Turner and Herbie Hancock haven't given up their careers as entertainers since finding Soka Gakkai and Nichiren Buddhism.

Perhaps the takeaway is binary thinking is unskillful, that there are no purely black and white lines to help you determine what is and is not Right Livelihood.

To further complicate matters, Ajaan Suwat Suvaco strikes are rather absolutist chord in his explanation of how practicing Right Livelihood is critical to developing Right Concentration:

> As for Right Livelihood, you set your mind on providing for your livelihood exclusively in a right way. You're firm in not making a livelihood in ways that are wrong, not acting in ways that are wrong, not speaking in ways that are corrupt and wrong. You won't make any effort in ways that go off the path, you won't be mindful in ways that lie outside the path. You'll keep being mindful in ways that stay on the path. You make this vow to yourself as a firm determination. This is one level of establishing the mind rightly."

What Ajaan Suwat Suvaco is saying is correct, but I don't think he's saying that one must completely and immediately abandon all forms of Wrong Livelihood with the snap of a finger. Buddhism is not, in my experience, a Big Bang; the Buddha was quite deliberate in describing it as a path. And as a path, as we follow it, we change, we mature, we gain deeper understanding.

What of you and your career? Are there occasions in your job when you realize that maybe your actions or someone else's actions in the company don't quite comport with the practice, even though the action is completely legal and ethical from a business perspective? If you do have those moments of doubt, that is a good thing; it means you have been faithfully practicing. But it doesn't mean you must immediately quit or look for other work. Rather, it means you have something to contemplate during your next meditation session.

13

Right Effort

THE SINGLE LIFE CAN BE SO DREARY and stressful at the same time – alas, what is a poor gay boy to do? Striking the right balance can be so difficult. Endlessly checking Grindr or Jack'd for new cute faces leads more frequently than not to disappointing meetings and meaningless hookups that, when looking back, really weren't very satisfying.

It's enough to make you renounce the dating life altogether and retreat to the solitary life of, what? Perusing Internet porn? Watching *Glee* reruns? Fantasizing that you're in the *Amazing Race*? Maybe there's a new Vietnamese restaurant I could check out. I got it, I'll go buy something!

It's like being on the dance floor between songs, during that period when there is no real melody and the back beat is transitioning. Do I just stand here and wait for the song to start? Do I dance a bit to the backbeat, uncertain of where it might go? Do I just go get a drink?

Actually, I think it's more I am like a guitar with strings that are either too loose or too tight, never playable or in tune. Wait, that sounds so familiar, like something the Buddha would say.

Don't faint or start thinking that I've lost my mind. I know what you're thinking: What has the Buddha ever said about the gay dating scene? Nothing specific perhaps, but if you take a look at the *Sona Sutta*, the Buddha uses a very interesting metaphor.

Sona was a monk who exerted himself so intensely in his meditation practice that one time he had done walking meditation for so long that the soles of his feet were cracked and bleeding. He sat for some more meditation when the thought occurred to him something like this: "You know, I'm not getting much out of this monastic scene, there are still so many things I want. Why don't I just chuck it all and go back home? I can still support the Sangha, plus enjoy a more comfortable life."

Well, the Buddha became aware of this so he teleported himself to Sona's side where he asked the monk, "Dude, what are you thinking?"

The Buddha then uses a metaphor involving a vina, a stringed instrument, to help Sona understand how to balance his efforts. If the strings are too tight, the instrument is unplayable. If the strings are too loose, the instrument is unplayable. Only when effort is exerted to find just the right string tension will the instrument be playable.

If you noticed, this sort of Goldilocks state of tension with the vina strings is right in the middle: not too tight, not too loose, but just right.

OK, I know what you're thinking – what has this got to do with finding a boyfriend? Probably not much. Or maybe everything. But the real point is when our lives feel out of sorts, it may be from a lack of proper concentration, and to regain proper concentration, we must put forth the Right Effort.

Wow, aren't I clever? I managed to turn the topic of gay dating into one about the Noble Eightfold Path!

But seriously, just about every time I feel like my life is a bit disconnected, I can trace the problem back to my meditation practice. While I seldom have gone to the extreme of meditating so much that my ass is sore, there are times when my practice becomes so lax that I go for days without even getting ten minutes in. And what the Buddha was telling Soma was the right method, the Right Effort, was in the middle.

The notion of Right Effort is part of the concentration group in the Noble Eightfold Path. Among the key elements of Right Effort are the Four Right Efforts. These are:

1. Develop skillful actions that one does not already possess
2. Further develop skillful actions one already possesses so they become more refined
3. Abandon unskillful actions one already has
4. Prevent the development of unskillful actions that one does not have

In other words, strengthen whatever qualities you have that make you a decent person and a good date, work on developing other qualities that would make you an even better person and date, work on getting rid of those qualities that annoy people, and make sure you don't develop any new negative qualities that limit your dating prospects.

Think of it this way: if you're not aware of the things you do that bug people or make you less attractive to people, you'll continue to lose on the dating front. And on a more serious note, if you're always worried about what you do, how others perceive you, or continuously worry as to why people don't want to date you, then you will be distracted and restless whenever you attempt to meditate.

Now, clearly, exerting the Right Effort is important for a lot of things, not just dating. Right Effort is vitally important to living a satisfying and happy life.

Right Effort is required to develop disciplined concentration, and our most serious impediment to our efforts at concentration is all of the unskillful things we do that bring us regret or confusion, or just plain restlessness.

It goes back to thinking about our practice as if it were a three-legged stool: each leg represents either Wisdom, Virtue, or Concentration. We need to refine our virtue to be able to concentrate during mediation without distraction by the things we've said or done, and when we achieve proper concentration, we start to develop wisdom that helps us further strengthen our virtue. Of course, before any of that is possible, we need at least wisdom enough to know what virtue is and how to get started.

So it's back to the cushion for me with a bit more regularity. Remember, overdoing it can be just as bad as not doing it at all. And finding that balance in anything takes effort – the Right Effort.

14

Right Mindfulness

MINDFULNESS IS ONE OF THOSE UBIQUITOUS TERMS that has entered pop culture and become so mainstream it's lost much of its oomph. There's a plethora of webinars, seminars, retreats, self-help books, and authors making the circuit extolling the virtues of mindfulness and the fruits of its practice. It gets trotted out like a pretty pony, a panacea to help you become a better student, better business person, make more money, a better worker, maybe even a better artist, musician, doctor, lawyer, sex worker.

Huh? What?

Exactly. In its simplest form, mindfulness is merely paying attention and developing focus in your awareness. Often, we experience unpleasant events because we haven't been paying attention, and when we work hard to prepare for something, we at times miss opportunities for the same reason.

The refrain in a Scissor Sisters song exemplifies what I mean.

> It can't come quickly enough
> And now you've spent your life
> Waiting for this moment
> And when you finally saw it come
> It passed you by and left you so defeated

What did the Buddha say about mindfulness? Let me modernize an analogy he used in the *Samyutta Nikāya*. (You can find the original sutta in the SN 47.20 if you want to look it up.)

There's a throng of people in a gay bar featuring male go-go dancers. The dancers are all hot boys, their bodies clad only with bikini briefs as they gyrate and shake to the thumping sound of house music blaring throughout the bar. The men watching the dancers are cheering, walking up to the dancers with cash to seductively place into their skimpy underwear. Everyone is ordering drinks.

You, on the other hand, are a server in this bar delivering those drinks amongst the throng. You carefully balance them on your tray as you negotiate your way through the crowd, focused on not spilling any of them because no one wants a sticky glass with their cosmo. You can't be distracted by the dancers; instead you're hyper aware of the bumping, bumbling bodies around you as you make your way to your destination, where you deliver the drinks undisturbed and receive a nice tip.

You are being mindful of the task at hand, mindful of where your body is in relation to everyone else, mindful of the drinks on your tray, hardly noticing the music in the background.

This is a very basic – mundane if you will – form of mindfulness. So is the type of mindfulness you would develop to improve your job performance, or your studying habits, or to become a better golfer. It's a start, but it's not the type of mindfulness the Buddha said you need to become a better person, to become harmless, and for developing compassion.

Remember the Eightfold Path is cumulative. You start with Right View, and build from there. While mindfulness training can help you become more successful, the focus is on self-gratification, and this can mean being successful at the expense of others. And that's not Right View.

It's neither Right Intention nor Right Livelihood as well. But it's a start.

But to really get a handle on Right Mindfulness, you need to focus on the right things. This mundane mindfulness I mention really doesn't get you anywhere. Awful people can be very mindful. Developing true Right Mindfulness, however, will bring you an insight so profound that you'll never look at the world the same again.

It begins and ends with meditation. While it is possible to meditate regularly and not be Buddhist, you cannot be Buddhist without regularly meditating. There are many books and pamphlets on a wide variety of meditation techniques, but they're not all equal. Even the most important sutta in the Pali canon regarding mindfulness – the *Satipatthana Sutta* – can seem overwhelmingly complicated as it lays out the skillful "things" to meditate on.

For example, even the simplest technique can create confusion: Contemplating the Breath. What does that mean? And then there's the idea of avoiding distracting thoughts as you meditate. Does that mean you don't think? How do you not think?

That was a big hang-up for me when I first began meditating. I thought the idea was to stop all my thinking, but when I tried that, I would get super frustrated because I kept thinking about not thinking!

A common metaphor in Southeast Asia for teaching mindfulness uses taming an elephant as the example. And also, a common metaphor for how the mind jumps about from one thought to the next is a monkey. In fact, in Asia an untrained mind is often referred to as the monkey mind.

For many of us in the West, taming an elephant is an unfamiliar task, and the "monkey mind" may not be as meaningful for us. But, we've all probably seen at least one Western film before, and are probably familiar with breaking a horse. And we've certainly all seen squirrels.

How many times have you been in a vehicle and up ahead saw a squirrel by the side of the road? The squirrel is skittish, hesitant. Should it cross the road now? Should it wait? It runs out into the street, stops, runs back, then runs out in the street again. It is super distracted, not sure which way to go and then SPLAT! The squirrel gets run over because it couldn't make up its mind and act appropriately.

Your untrained mind is very much like the indecisive squirrel. The untrained mind has difficultly staying focused, is easily distracted, and will chase random thoughts. We could very easily end up like the squirrel and walk into traffic without paying attention and get run over. Or we could be reading something and suddenly our mind gets triggered into a random thought, yet our eyes continue to scan the page before us until we eventually return to the book and realize we have no idea what we just read.

We need to train our mind to remain fixed on an object, which in this case simply means what we're paying attention to. It's like breaking a horse. Your mind may be your own mind, you think, but you don't really control it. For years you've basically let it operate on its own, "without thinking."

Like a wild horse that needs to be trained to accept a rider who will then direct the horse to do what the rider wants it to do, your mind needs to be trained so that you can direct it to pay attention to fruitful subjects without distraction.

When breaking a horse, you start with a very simple but important task: you rope the horse and bring it under your control. And in that process, you wait until the beast settles down and stops fighting you. Once that's achieved, the next step might be getting it used to having a blanket on, and then a saddle, and eventually, you get in that saddle and work on controlling the horse, making it do what you want it to do.

But the horse rebels and knocks you off! So, as they say, you brush the dirt off yourself and get right back into the saddle until eventually the horse acquiesces to your commands.

Your mind reacts the same way when you attempt to keep it focused on one thing. And not only focused on one thing, but sustained focus. And I'm here to tell you, your mind will resist.

So let's get you started on some basics. First, sit your ass down.

You don't have to sit in a lotus position. Simply sitting cross-legged is fine, but you should sit on a cushion or something similar to raise your butt higher than your feet. And if sitting on a cushion is too uncomfortable, sitting in a firm chair works. Just make it a hard chair, not a comfy chair. You don't want to fall asleep.

Select a quiet room in your home. Remove all distractions. Turn your phone off (unless you're using one of those meditation apps to keep time). Lay your hands in your lap, palms up. Find what feels natural for you. For most right-handed people, you will feel more comfortable with your left hand under your right.

Sit erect. If you're in a chair, avoid leaning into the back of the chair. And if you're in a chair, keep your legs separated, not crossed at the ankle. Best if your legs are bent at right angles with your heels directly under your knees.

Now breath in through your nose. Feel the air as it goes by your nostrils. Avoid following the flow of air into your lungs. Some say your nostrils are the gate, and gatekeepers merely observe who goes in and out of the gate – the gatekeeper does not follow anyone, just watches them go in and out.

So breath in, then breath out. Be aware you are breathing in, and be aware you are breathing out. Focus your attention on the fact that you breathe in, and then you breathe out. You can even mentally say, "breathe in ... breathe out," and so on.

Sooner or later, probably with the third breath, but it might even be sooner, your mind will go, "What's that noise?" Or some random thought will flow into your awareness. This happens to everyone. This is also when I made the rookie mistake of trying to force these thoughts out of my mind. But that's not what you should do. Rather, become aware of that random thought. You might even say with your mind's voice, "What is that thought? Where did it come from?" Just by doing that, the random thought will disappear, allowing you to return your focus on your breath.

It's kind of like a law of mental physics. Just as two objects cannot occupy the same space simultaneously, you cannot think two thoughts simultaneously. So by responding to a random thought with, "What is that thought? Where did it come from?" you bump the thought out of your mind and you can return to your breath.

This will happen over and over and over and over. Meditation takes persistence. So it helps to start with short time periods, even as short as just 5 minutes for each session. Then increase it to 10 minutes, and as that feels comfortable, increase it to 15, then 20, and on until you reach a comfortable length of time. I generally meditate for 20 minutes. On special occasions I may go for longer periods.

But the actual length of time you spend meditating isn't as important as the length of time you can go without having to respond to a random thought that breaks your concentration. Remember, the horse doesn't let you ride it the first time your try.

This is where all the earlier items in the Noble Eightfold Path come into play. The more you practice Right View, Right Speech, and Right Livelihood, for example, the less anxious you become because you're not worried about how you might have hurt someone or screwed someone over, and that helps your concentration.

Once you are able to sustain attention on your breath – and that could take days, or weeks, or months, or even years, don't lose heart – you'll be ready to contemplate "objects" other than the breath. Such as contemplating that your body is not you and you are not your body. Your body ages, and there's nothing you can do about it, because you are not your body, and your body is not you.

While this may sound odd, believe it or not, with sustained practice you will reach a point where you can more effectively discern not only what you are doing in the present moment, but what your true intentions are for acting in the manner you choose. You will develop greater compassion for others, even when they do annoying things.

Will you stop being angry? Not necessarily. But you will become more aware of your anger and what triggers it so you can anticipate it and manage it more effectively.

Will you stop feeling sad? No, but you'll better understand how feelings are transient, and you will be able to disengage from them so you don't dwell on negative feelings or thoughts.

Does it mean you become emotionless? Not at all! You learn to experience emotions for what they are and let them pass.

Does it mean no one will ever break your heart again? Definitely not. As long as we continue to make attachments to others, those attachments will break and sometimes they hurt. But again, we learn how to avoid dwelling in the hurt.

Read the *Satipatthana Sutta* to see all the meditation techniques the Buddha recommended.

15

Right Concentration

IF RIGHT MINDFULNESS IS TRAINING THE MIND to be fully aware of what is happening right now, developing that raw awareness of the now without interference from what happened in the past or what is anticipated in the future, then Right Concentration is skillfully using such a mind to evaluate and come to terms with how things really are.

Let that sink in for a moment – seeing things as they really are. Because when you can do that, your mind, your entire being, will be liberated.

"Come on, I already know how things really are, I already know how jaded and duplicitous people can be."

Sorry sweetie, that's not seeing things as they really are. Any deluded mind can understand how other deluded minds operate and get along with each other.

Because I am not so advanced, the best I can describe what it means to see things as they really are is to say it's an experience, not knowledge, and the more you try to put it into words, the further away you are from really understanding it.

For good or ill, it's very much like an LSD trip in that the awareness and "understanding" you experience in an acid trip cannot be explained in words. Anyone who has tried to do this knows the frustration experienced by the limits of language.

Of course, there are Buddhist purists who will look at what I just wrote and say I don't know what I'm talking about. They would discredit me for seeming to endorse hallucinogens as a shortcut to Nibbana. But there is a body of research out there, including scientific data, showing what's going on in our brain during an LSD trip is nearly identical with what goes on in our brain during deep states of meditation.

The nice thing about meditation is you aren't going to be arrested and sent to prison for doing it. And once you learn the technique, you can do it on your own without much additional guidance.

As you can see, meditation is critical to developing both Right Mindfulness and Right Concentration. Consider these wise words from Thanissaro Bhikkhu in the article "The Path of Concentration and Mindfulness," from the website Access to Insight:

> Every time (the Buddha) explains mindfulness and its place in the path, he makes it clear that the purpose of mindfulness practice is to lead the mind into a state of Right Concentration – to get the mind to settle down and to find a place where it can really feel stable, at home, where it can look at things steadily and see them for what they are.

Thanissaro Bhikkhu further explains that developing Right Concentration isn't this odious task that is described by other practitioners and in other Buddhist literature. In fact, it's blissful, even pleasurable. So despite not necessarily being "easy," it's not a drag.

Perhaps it's because many teachers and other practitioners talk about Right Concentration being synonymous with Jhana.

"Jhana say what?"

It's amusing at times how folks freak out over the specificity of certain terms and use that as an excuse not to examine or explore something further, and yet won't hesitate to correct you if you happen to say "shade" when you should have said "read," which actually is very nuanced and more difficult at times to discern the difference between the two than you may think.

But, yes, the Buddha does talk about the jhanas when discussing Right Concentration, and the descriptions are pretty simple. I cannot say for certain, but I have experienced moments during meditation that may have been what it known as the First Jhana. They are fleeting moments of pure oneness that quickly disappear as soon as I think to myself, "Wow, what is that?"

So let's attempt to demystify this a bit and talk about the jhanas, because they are very important. You needn't spend a lot of time reading the traditional Buddhist canon to discover the term "jhana" is mentioned a lot. And the path to true liberation goes right through the jhanas.

Meditation is critical here. We'll talk about meditative techniques and practice later. But for now we really need to lay the groundwork as to meditation's critical role in this process. And to make things a bit easier, we'll start off with describing the two basic types of mediation: meditation that develops serenity and meditation that develops insight. The latter is absolutely necessary to Right Concentration, but the former is necessary to still the mind enough to become skillfully concentrated.

Think of it this way: developing serenity of mind will help you achieve the type of concentration you will need to gain the wisdom you'll need to see things as they really are. However, there are obstacles you will encounter as you practice meditation. Fortunately, these obstacles have common characteristics and common solutions and have been nicely categorized as the Five Hindrances. Overcoming the Five Hindrances is the *sine qua non* of attaining Right Concentration.

The Five Hindrances are:

1. Sensual desire
2. Ill-will
3. Sloth and torpor
4. Restlessness and remorse
5. Doubt

The Buddha was very clear about how important overcoming these hindrances is to achieving freedom, as shown in this passage from the *Anguttara Nikāya*:

> One whose heart is overwhelmed by unrestrained covetousness will do what he should not do and neglect what he ought to do. And through that, his good name and his happiness will come to ruin.
>
> One whose heart is overwhelmed by ill-will ... by sloth and torpor ... by restlessness and remorse ... by skeptical doubt will do what he should not do and neglect what he ought to do. And through that, his good name and his happiness will come to ruin.
>
> But if a noble disciple has seen these five as defilements of the mind, he will give them up. And doing so, he is regarded as one of great wisdom, of abundant wisdom, clear-visioned, well endowed with wisdom. This is called "endowment with wisdom."

That line – "*But if a noble disciple has seen these five as defilements of the mind, he will give them up.*" – is very important, because for most of us, we don't see these as "defilements." In fact, we really don't see them at all or understand how they operate.

Also, it's important to keep in mind this doesn't necessarily mean giving up the material ways of the world entirely. Re-read this line: "*One whose heart is overwhelmed by unrestrained covetousness will do what he should not do and neglect what he ought to do. And through that, his good name and his happiness will come to ruin.*" For many of us, just keeping in mind that "unrestrained covetousness" is harmful in many ways will help us enormously as we proceed down the path. If we find that we do wish to renounce the world and its material ways, we can.

But it's not mandatory.

What is mandatory is understanding clearly how we are often unconsciously led through life by the nose, like an ox with a nose ring, by these unrestrained desires and thoughts, delivering us frequently to ambiguous and unsatisfying situations and outcomes.

Overcoming the Five Hindrances is accomplished by developing their opposites using the technique described in the Four Right Efforts. Remember these? Among the Four Right Efforts is being able to identify negative qualities within ourselves and work toward eliminating these qualities. This means taking dead aim at the Five Hindrances.

Let's cover each of the Five Hindrances and how to overcome them individually.

Sensual desire includes everything from desiring, thinking about, and having sex to wanting comfort and nice things in our life. It's the desire for things, thoughts, and activities that please us and make us feel good. There is a strong biological basis for this, which makes overcoming and subduing these desires a significant challenge. When we experience pleasure, or anticipate pleasure, our brain chemistry becomes altered. This is why it is so difficult at times to resist certain activities, whether it's flirting with someone with hopes of bedding him, viewing porn, or even something as simple as avoiding carbs like French fries in your diet.

We strengthen this biological hold on us by giving frequent attention to our sensual desires and activities. Fortunately, the Buddha has a relatively straightforward strategy for combating this desire, and that's paying attention to the disgusting. For example, distracted by a hot guy on the street and find yourself thinking about what you'd do with him once you got him in bed? What if you pictured him not as a handsome naked hunk in your sheets, but as a corpse with the skin peeled off?

"Holy shite! WTF are you talking about?"

Exactly. To overcome distraction from what we consider beautiful and desirable, think of it as hideous and repugnant. During meditation, even, we can "contemplate the body" as it is: bones, blood, ligaments, organs, ooze, pus, excrement – all the things a body truly is, but we never think about because it disgusts us. Eventually, we learn to see a body just as a body because we have seen what happens to a body. We have restrained our desires. We don't have to eliminate them entirely, just keep a lid on them.

Ill-will is exactly what it sounds like, a desire for something bad to happen to others who anger us or who we believe have wronged us. This one is challenging. Because sometimes, we turn this ill-will on ourselves. We become our harshest critic and our own worst bully. Negative thinking becomes a pattern that rewards itself by being self-congratulatory.

We are not our minds. As one of the aggregates, our minds are not "self." Which means we can train our minds to have different thinking processes. Some may need therapeutic assistance with this. There's nothing wrong with that. But the Buddha has a practice that can help overcome ill-will, and that's called the Loving Kindness Meditation. I chant this after each meditation session, starting first with expressing kindness and compassion for myself:

> May I be free from hatred; may I be free from oppression; may I be free from troubles; may my happiness be protected; may I be happy.

I then similarly chant expressing the same kindness and compassion for all beings, human and animal, no one specifically in mind:

> May all beings be free from hatred; may all beings be free from oppression; may all beings be free from troubles; may all beings be free from suffering; may all beings be happy.

We start with ourselves because as mentioned earlier, we can often be our own worst bully. And besides, we can't truly show compassion and empathy for others without first genuinely showing it for ourselves. Then we move on to the vague category of all other sentient beings. After practicing this for a while, you will feel a change; you won't feel like you're just repeating words and, instead, start to feel as though you really mean and intend what you're saying.

That's when it's time to start adding specific people to the chant and meditation, beginning first with people you like. The people we like and love can still disappoint us and anger us, but it's easier for us to wish them well because we like them

Next, we add neutral specific people, people we neither particularly like nor dislike, such as co-workers, people we see with some frequency but may not know well ,such as restaurant servers, store clerks, and so on.

Once we feel the compassion and empathy build for them, the we can add people we truly dislike. At first, we have probably wished bad things to happen to them. That's ill-will, but through developing compassion, we stop desiring bad things to happen and begin to desire they overcome their own suffering. This is the most difficult loving kindness to develop; that's why we don't start with it. We have to work our way toward it.

Sloth and torpor sounds odd, but it's really quite simple. In terms of meditation, it means dozing off. This can be a significant hindrance to any meditation practice. The idea is to become ardent in your practice. And there are some very simple things to do to prevent sloth and torpor.

For one, know that what you eat before meditation can bring on drowsiness. I tend to do my sitting meditation early in the day before lunch, and sometimes before I even have breakfast. An empty stomach can be your friend, or if your belly grumbles so much it becomes distracting, eat small portions of food that won't make you drowsy.

Making sure you're getting enough sleep is important as well. And being aware of light. Sometimes it's recommended to meditate with your eyes open just a slit to let in light. But conjuring an image of a bright light can accomplish this as well.

As I mentioned, becoming "ardent" in your practice is important. This means being earnest about it, and one way of becoming ardent is to contemplate death. Seriously, remind yourself there's no guarantee that you will accomplish everything you want when you want it, because death waits on no one. Knowing that we could die before accomplishing something helps develop this ardency and motivates us into seriousness. Frequently, contemplation of death also helps with sensual desire.

We're not talking about becoming morbid or obsessed with death, merely recognizing its presence and inevitability. The younger you are, the more likely death is perceived as something far, far away. Change that perception. It wakes you up.

Restlessness and remorse represent interruptions in concentration brought on by anticipating the future or regretting past actions. Overcoming these is a process that requires daily practice.

For restlessness, start with clearing your mind of thoughts regarding any other tasks you know are coming up. Have plans in place, schedules for events, so your mind can rest and not worry what will happen next. Next, cultivate the mindset that there is only the now, the past is gone, the future not yet here. We are in the present moment we are because of all we've done in the past, and to ensure that our future is a pleasant one, we must pay attention to what we are doing right now, because what we're doing right now, regardless of what we did in the past, is shaping our future.

The more you can do this, any remorse you have for past actions will diminish as you develop the skill needed to act more skillfully in the future, reducing the likeliness of further remorse.

Developing skillful friendships is very important as well. Choosing friends who look out for you and who truly desire the best for you is very important to relieving anxiety and restlessness. If you're always wondering about a friend's motives or why they did something, this will distract your mind and prevent it from settling down.

It also helps to periodically read Dhamma. Set aside one day a week to read something from the canon and think about what you read and how it applies today. You can find most of the Tipitika online at Access to Insight; just Google it. Just stick with the core suttas and avoid reading material by specific "gurus" or other, prolific authors. For example, instead of reading what some other writer says about the *Heart Sutra*, read the sutra yourself. Contemplate it and develop your own understanding of it. And then talk about it with someone else who also has read it and with whom you feel comfortable. Avoid those who try to tell you how to think about it.

Consider this from the *Samyutta Nikāya*:

> If there is water in a pot, stirred by the wind, agitated, swaying and producing waves, a man with a normal faculty of sight could not properly recognize and see the image of his own face. In the same way, when one's mind is possessed by restlessness and remorse, overpowered by restlessness and remorse, one cannot properly see the escape from restlessness and remorse that have arisen; then one does not properly understand one's own welfare, nor that of another, nor that of both; and also texts memorized a long time ago do not come into one's mind, not to speak of those not memorized.

Doubt can afflict you as you begin to wonder whether all your efforts are worth it, whether you are making any progress, or even if the mind can ever be stilled. Fortunately, many of the methods used to overcome restlessness and remorse also work to overcome doubt, in particular Dhamma study and cultivating positive friendships. An encouraging friend can go a long way to helping you dispel the clouds of doubt.

Consider another very similar passage to the one above from the *Samyutta Nikāya*:

> If there is a pot of water which is turbid, stirred up and muddy, and this pot is put into a dark place, then a man with a normal faculty of sight could not properly recognize and see the image of his own face. In the same way, when one's mind is possessed by doubt,

overpowered by doubt, then one cannot properly see the escape from doubt which has arisen; then one does not properly understand one's own welfare, nor that of another, nor that of both; and also texts memorized a long time ago do not come into one's mind, not to speak of those not memorized."

Overcoming the Five Hindrances is a process, and the more skillful you become at your daily practice, the easier it gets. And the more settled your mind becomes, the greater the likelihood you will experience jhana.

While the Buddha speaks of the jhanas frequently throughout the Tipitika, the descriptions can appear daunting and very esoteric. But it's really much simpler than what you may think from reading the canon. When you can sustain your mind's focus, when your attention on your meditation object is clear and ardent and sustained to exclude distraction from random, extraneous thoughts, you will know it. The experience is blissful at first. Eventually you come to know it just as it is. It will no longer be this seemingly unattainable state of mind. And even during trying times of turmoil and even emotional pain, you will find it easier to remain steadfast with equanimity.

Part III

The Layperson's Path to Peace

16

Developing a Meditation Practice

WE'VE COVERED SOME BUDDHIST BASICS, including things like the Four Noble Truths, the Noble Eightfold Path, the Four Right Efforts, the Five Hindrances, and some others. Sounds like a lot. But the key to all this is developing and sustaining a regular meditation practice.

Easier said than done, but the irony is it's not that difficult.

My understanding of what is really supposed to be going on during meditation has gone through many transformations. Initially, I interpreted the notion of "stilling" or "quieting" the mind to mean I was supposed to stop all thinking, that I needed to turn off the internal chatter within my head. But that was only half right.

I was so focused on my breathing in an effort to force out all other thoughts that meditation became a chore; it was as though I was emulating Sisyphus trying to push a giant boulder up a mountainside. The endeavor was so exhausting that I often fell asleep during a sit.

Then I learned to quit fighting my thoughts, just let them pass by like a float in a parade. This helped immensely with the ever-present song or jingle that would pop into my head during meditation. In fact, I am seldom bothered any more by a song stuck in my mind while I sit. Staying focused on my breath is much easier now.

Still, for a long time it just didn't seem like I was getting anywhere. On occasion, some of my most satisfying sits involved some very specific thinking going on in my mind. It wasn't when I was floating in the absorption of my breath. In fact, this buoyant state of my mind remaining aloof from other mental activities was bringing on the sleepiness problem I had in the past. Rather, my most insightful moments in meditation actually involved me fixing my mind on a thought or concept and following that thought through in what seemed like logical increments. On the rare occasions when this occurred, I reached a level of understanding that was very satisfying about whatever it was I had been thinking. I might even say it was euphoric.

Having said that, my mind does tend to enjoy treading paths of thought that are self-indulgent and irrelevant. Yet, increasingly I have become intrigued by how the Buddha describes the First Jhana, as a state of "deliberate and sustained thought."

And then I read this extraordinary post at *The Theravadin*, an online Buddhist magazine. The author uses two very vivid – for me – metaphors to describe how meditation works.

In the first metaphor, *The Theravadin* uses a common behavior to describe how we develop the mindfulness necessary for effective meditation: learning how to ride a bike.

When first learning to ride a bike, we are very focused on maintaining balance so we can move forward, so focused on this single element that often – at least I remember doing this – we aren't looking ahead at what's coming and we run into other objects, like curbs or trees.

Seriously, I ran into a tree once when I was six while trying to ride an adult-size bicycle.

But with persistence, we develop the balance necessary to keep our bicycle upright. When that happens, we ride with ease, able to look around us at the scenery as we peddle along. We're still riding the bike, we're still doing everything we need to do to maintain balance, but we are no longer "aware" of that – it's automatic now.

It's such a brilliant metaphor because developing the balance necessary to ride a bicycle with ease is very much like developing a fixed mind in meditation. Finding the balance needed to ride a bicycle with ease is just like remaining fixed on a meditation object, such as the breath.

> Developing the jhanas is like learning how to ride a (mental) bike. When learning how to ride a bike there are two important things involved: First of all, you see others on the bike and see how much fun they have. You want that too. Secondly, almost everyone you see did learn it, so you are thinking: I can do it too. Third, when you are up on the bike, you learn to intuitively avoid falling – but that takes lot of practice. You know now, that the falling was actually part of the game, and it taught you how NOT to fall. In order to develop the skill to keep your balance your mind had to learn to avoid extreme movements away from the center. You also realized that eventually, once you started to keep going, the balance was easy to hold and the fun bike ride started.

Then *The Theravadin* introduces another powerful metaphor that really got my mind alert. Imagine being carried along by the powerful currents of a wild river. Out of sheer luck, you are able to grasp onto a rock. What are you going to do? You are going to cling to that rock with every ounce of energy you have, and if you are able, you will pull yourself out of the raging river onto the rock.

> The attainment of the jhana, according to this simile, is achieved by a "not-floating away" or "not-drifting-away." This is similar to a person in a wild river pushed along by the current who would try to hold on to a stone – long enough to pull himself out of the water and step on that stone. Such a temporary break (because he has not yet crossed the river but is still caught in the middle) on the steady rock in the middle of a wild river means also that no effort is necessary to maintain that calm position and one feels calmness and aloofness while the river/stream of the senses retreats.

Once up on that rock, what would you do? You have a moment of relative ease to collect your breath, re-focus your thoughts and contemplate your next move. You can't stay on that rock forever. At any moment, the raging river could send you a wave that will knock you off your perch. But it is, temporarily at least, a safe haven that allows you to determine how to extract yourself from this predicament.

Developing concentration is vital to meditation, but it isn't the end. Once you learn how to ride the bike, you need to learn how to enjoy the ride. And once you've pulled yourself out of the river onto the relative safety of a rock, you must contemplate your escape to complete safety. Standing on that rock forever is not the solution. It is merely the vantage point.

Before going on, let's cover a few meditation basics to get you started.

Begin small, but be punctual and persistent

Set aside at least one time during your day for meditation and keep the appointment. But don't make the session too long at first. One of the key obstacles in developing any type of new behavior is attempting to achieve everything all at once. I didn't write this book in one sitting. If I had tried that, I would have given up long ago out of frustration. So it is with meditation.

Begin with very short sessions, no more than five minutes duration, and if necessary, even shorter. But five minutes is a good place to start. And do your best to sit at about the same time each day. Make it a habit. Put it in your schedule or your calendar. Set reminders if you need to. And as you become more consistent, you will know the right moment to slowly add time to your sessions.

But don't be afraid to cut a session short even if you've already worked your way to longer sessions. If you find yourself struggling during a session, give it up and stop. Perhaps something in the next section is interfering with your stately repose.

Anticipate interruptions and remove them

I used to have cats. There's nothing like settling into a meditation session only to be disturbed by forlorn meowing. There were times too when one or both of my cats would want to get into my lap. The meowing I could ward off with some planning, and their desire to get into my lap I learned to deal with.

Why does a cat meow? Sometimes because it's hungry, lonely, or the litter box needs cleaning. So before I would begin a session, I would make sure there was food in their bowl and clean water available in their dish. To avoid loneliness, I would give them attention and affection prior to the session and this usually calmed them so they could settle down and fall asleep somewhere else. And, of course, I cleaned their box before I began to meditate.

Over time, they learned to mostly ignore me while I sat. When they attempted to sit in my lap, my hands resting in my lap mostly dissuaded them, but if they persisted, it became part of the session. "What is that pawing at me? It's the cat. Return to the breath. Breathe in. Breathe out." The cat walks away.

I also clear my mind of other tasks. If there is something I need to do later, I schedule that activity so I don't need to think about it. I search my mind to identify anything I may have forgotten; if I need to address that item immediately, I do so it doesn't linger in the back of my mind. Otherwise, I schedule a time later to work on that task.

I don't turn off my phone because I use a meditation app to time my session, but if you use another method to time your session, you can turn off the phone so it doesn't interrupt you. I will put the "do not disturb" function on so other message notifications don't interrupt me. The idea is to remove those interruptions that arise in your mind, and that usually involves tasks you need to complete.

But there is another interruption of mind that can arise that can only be eliminated through "good living." In other words, you need to be acting throughout the day in a manner that doesn't create ill will with others. Did you speak harshly to someone earlier? Or did someone say something to you that is nagging at your mind? Maybe because of something you said or did in the past?

This type of interruption takes time to eliminate, but eventually you can reduce them by living daily in a manner that respects others and is considerate of others' feelings. And not just people you know, but strangers too.

Sit in a manner you can sustain and in the same spot each time

Being in the same room or same general area each time is important at first. As you get more comfortable with practice, you'll find you can do it almost anywhere.

How you sit is not as important as others may make you think. Some may say you must sit in a lotus position, or that you must at least sit cross-legged. If you can do so comfortably, then fine, sit in a full lotus or cross-legged position. Put a cushion or two under you so that your butt is raised up higher than your feet.

However, not everyone is limber enough to do this, and as you grow older, sitting on the floor may become too difficult and unmanageable. For example, I sit in a chair. Not a comfy chair, mind you, but a stiff, kitchen-type chair. And I don't lean into the back of the chair; I sit erect to keep my back away from the back of the chair. I place my feet flat on the floor in front of me with my knees at right angles. I do not cross my feet at my ankles. You can even try a kneeling chair.

Place your hands in your lap, palms up. For most, if you're right-handed, it will feel more comfortable to place your right hand into the palm of your left hand, and vice versa if you're left-handed. Regardless, find that natural position for your hands so they "feel" as though they are in the right place.

Now relax, but remain upright and avoid slouching. It's time to begin focusing on your "object."

Start with the breath as your first meditation object

Meditation is a technique to train your mind to remain focused on thoughts and objects that help you understand better how things really are. But for most of us, this is a significant challenge because while we may think we control our minds, we really don't. That's because we are not our minds, and our minds are not who we are. For now, "who we are" is irrelevant. For now, the task is to train our minds to attend to useful tasks and objects, to submit to our will, if that helps, rather than allowing our mind to take us willy-nilly where it wants to go.

So we start with the breath. It's a very simple object because it's always there. If we aren't breathing, we're dead . We breathe without thinking about it, and as such, it's a very useful meditation object.

But we don't want to "follow" the breath, because we might get lost and fall asleep. Start by mentally saying to yourself as you breathe in, "breathe in." And as you breathe out, "breathe out." Just that. Avoid saying "I am breathing in," because as soon as you say "I" you are engaging the ego, and our goal is to remove the ego. So it's just, "Breathe in, Breathe out."

As you do this, be aware of the air passing through your nostrils, and that's as far as you go. Feel the air passing your nostrils, but don't follow it through your nose and into your lungs. Think of the entrance to your nose as the gate to a city. You are the gatekeeper. A gatekeeper only sees who comes in and who goes out. The gatekeeper doesn't follow who comes in to see where they go, nor does the gatekeeper follow who leaves the city to see where they are headed. The gatekeeper only sees who comes in and who goes out.

Breathe in, breathe out. That is your object. That is what you want your mind to attend to, but your mind will soon rebel.

A thought will occur to you. Or you'll hear a sound. Or you'll feel a sensation in your foot, or lower back, or there will be an itch behind your ear.

Your mind is bored. It doesn't like having to remain focused on the breath. So it attempts to create distractions. Yes, your mind has a "mind" of its own, and we've let it do whatever it wants for so long, it doesn't react submissively when we decide to train it to do what we want.

These distractions are actually a handy way for you to learn to understand sensations for what they really are. So avoid becoming frustrated. Rather, recognize the thought or sensation simply as a thought or sensation, and your fixation on this "distracting object" will disappear and you can return to your breath.

That's what thoughts are. That's what sensations are. That's what perceptions are. They are objects the mind wants to grasp and hold on to and avoid paying attention to what is going on right now, in this moment. Without a trained mind, we can make inappropriate decisions based on distracting stimuli. We lose the ability to think through the logical outcome should we follow a particular path of activity, which often leads us to results that baffle us.

How then, you may ask, do you recognize a distraction without focusing on it?

When we begin meditation, we quickly realize random thoughts pop up in our minds without any relevance or even logic to them. Normally, we chase that thought or mental image down a rabbit hole and suddenly we're caught up in some mental fantasy. Instead of chasing the thought, try to identify where it came from. Focus on the thought itself, rather than its content.

"What is that? Where did that thought come from?"

When we do that, invariably, the thought disappears. When it's a sound, such as a siren in the background, instead of thinking, "Oh, a siren, I wonder if it's the police or an ambulance. Maybe it's a fire," simply recognize it as "sound." Because that's all it is. A sound. Any story your mind wants to weave around that sound is not the sound. Recognize it as merely "sound." And then return to your breath.

This will happen dozens of times during your early sessions, which is why we keep them short at the start. But with persistence, you will experience longer periods of sustained focus on your breathe with fewer mental interruptions and you will be able to gradually extend your meditation time.

Other methods to focus on breath

There are other ways to sustain focus on the breath beyond mentally saying, "breathe in, breathe out." One is reciting the word Budho. With this technique, you separate the word into its syllables and when breathing in, mentally say "Bud," which is pronounced more like "bood," and as you breathe out, mentally say "Ho." You still continue to focus on breath feeling it on your nostrils.

Counting is another method. Mentally you say "one" as you inhale, "two" as you exhale, and so on until you reach five. That's when you start to count down back to one. You do not count beyond five because the mind will wander and you will lose count and then lose concentration. You could even fall asleep.

Walking Meditation

I have always been intrigued by walking meditation. And when I received useful guidance on how to do this, it became an amazing experience. I strongly recommend you give it a try as you develop your skills with seated meditation.

Initially when I tried walking meditation, I always felt like I wasn't doing it properly. There are publications that describe it, provide some guidance, but for me, this was for me a situation where reading a book wasn't helping. I needed someone to show me.

That someone appeared several years ago when I made my second visit to a Thai temple in Chicago, Wat Phrasriratanamahadhatu, a Theravada Buddhist temple in the Uptown neighborhood. The Sunday activities are mostly social with some food offerings made to the monks for the alms round, as well as offerings of personal supplies. There's a big feast as well, a Sunday buffet of homemade Thai food. But that's another topic.

After I had finished helping clean up in the kitchen, one of the monks caught me and asked if I wanted to join some of them for meditation. Of course! So we went to another building (the temple has three buildings now) where they conduct classes and meditation. The monk explained that they start with walking meditation: had I ever done that?

Despite a few feeble attempts at the practice in the past, I said no. The monk gave me some personal instruction to get me started, which I must say was extraordinarily helpful. My experience with the practice that time was unlike any previous. Here's what he taught me.

Step one: Adopt a standing posture with hands held in front or behind the back (I held mine in front). Close the eyes while standing still and be aware of your posture while standing, running the mind's gaze on the body from the top of the head down to the feet, then back up, back down, back up, and back down. I did this with each pass timed with my breathing, fixing my awareness on the "object" of "standing." Not "I am standing." Just "standing."

Step two: Open the eyes and begin taking a step to initiate walking, focusing the mind on awareness of each step, realizing the various stages of pressure and lack of pressure on the feet as each step is made. At first, the stride of my steps was too long. I found that the walking was not only easier, but my mind sustained focus more effectively when I took smaller steps, each foot landing only just in front of the other. I keep my gaze downward but ahead of me, not at my feet or the floor directly in front of me.

Step three: Know you are walking. My awareness of each step was really quite extraordinary; I was focused and aware of how the floor felt on the sole of the left foot as it rocked with the shifting body weight, as well as aware of what the right foot was doing as it moved forward. There were moments of wavering balance, as I have arthritis in my right ankle, so when lifting the left foot, sometimes I wobbled as the body's weight shifted entirely to the right foot. But taking small, very deliberate steps took care of this.

Step four: When the other side of the room is reached, stand still, close the eyes, and bring awareness back to "standing." Just like I did at the start. It kept the mind from anticipating what was going to happen next, as I always had a task.

Step five: Open the eyes and focus on "turning," slowly turning the body around by taking small steps to the right, rotating the body in four "points;" so if my starting position was north, I first turn to the northeast, then east, then southeast, then south; all quite slowly and deliberately keeping my attention focused on "turning."

Step six: Close the eyes and go through the process of focusing the mind once again on "standing." Then resume the procedure by walking back to the other side of the room, repeating the process for the duration.

It was a wonderful experience, probably due to being a beginner. My attention was so well-focused that I really felt settled when we were through. I don't think I could do this effectively at home because where I now live I don't have enough space. But when I find myself in a location where I can do it, such as a park, I will slowly walk back and forth, ever mindful of each step I take.

Chanting as a Meditative Practice

A final topic to mention in regards to meditation is chanting.

Years ago I was at a celebration at the first temple I attended when a group of visiting monks had arrived for the festivities. Part of the day included chanting. While I had heard chanting on television shows about Buddhism, I had not, until that day, experienced it "live."

It was an awesome experience.

Interestingly, I also love Gregorian chant. And while I have not attempted to recite Latin chants, I have dabbled in Buddhist chanting. Listening to those monks – as well as the other temple members already familiar with chanting – reciting these ancient words in beautiful, sonorous voices was almost transcendent.

I can remember the Abbot explaining to the newcomers that they needn't worry if they couldn't follow the Pali text of the chant, copies of which were distributed among the group. Just sit back, he said, relax and meditate on the sound of the voices. Let your mind become calm, he said, while listening to the chanting. And it was true, just sitting there listening brought my mind to a stillness and focus that I seldom am able to attain during my regular sitting meditation.

I wanted to learn how to do this myself. I managed to pick up the easy parts, the phrases that were repeated plenty of times, such as, "Namo tassa bhagavato arahato samma-sambuddhassa."

This is part of the Refuge chant that includes this repeated part that I was able to learn as well:

> Buddham saranam gacchami.
> > I go to the Buddha for refuge.
> Dhammam saranam gacchami.
> > I go to the Dhamma for refuge.
> Sangham saranam gacchami.
> > I go to the Sangha for refuge.
>
> Dutiyampi buddham saranam gacchami.
> > A second time, I go to the Buddha for refuge.
> Dutiyampi dhammam saranam gacchami.
> > A second time, I go to the Dhamma for refuge.
> Dutiyampi sangham saranam gacchami.
> > A second time, I go to the Sangha for refuge.

> Tatiyampi buddham saranam gacchami.
> > A third time, I go to the Buddha for refuge.
> Tatiyampi dhammam saranam gacchami.
> > A third time, I go to the Dhamma for refuge.
> Tatiyampi sangham saranam gacchami.
> > A third time, I go to the Sangha for refuge.

More recently, I learned a new chant from another Buddhist group that I have found equally as soothing. This group chants, Nam Myoho Renge Kyo. I had to laugh to myself when I first heard the words to this chant, because there are so many episodes from the British sit-com *Absolutely Fabulous* during which Edina Monsoon butchers this chant as she attempts to recite it in her uniquely hedonistic and totally self-centered way.

Interestingly, a member of this particular group, which is affiliated with Soka Gakkai International, gave a brief explanation of the chant, saying that a scientist had become interested in it because the sound created by the chant was something that could be found in nature, in space.

I know what some of you are probably thinking: "Yeah, right, I bet it is." But that was not my reaction. I found nothing absurd about this man's explanation, and here's why.

Among the things I am passionate about, Buddhism being just one, is Frank Zappa. I had a blog about Frank Zappa's recordings. What, you may ask, has Frank Zappa got to do with Buddhist chanting? Not much, to be honest with you, although among the many religions he studied and poured over as a teen in the 1950s was Buddhism. But that's not where I'm going. In doing the background research for my blog entry on the album *Lumpy Gravy*, I found something very interesting.

Among the random conversations recorded for this album is a brief discourse when someone talks about the "big note." Here's the relevant portion of this seemingly inane soliloquy (picture this being said by a complete stoner, who most people would look at and think, "This guy's an idiot."):

> Everything in the universe is, is, is made of one element, which is a note, a single note. Atoms are really vibrations, you know. Which are extensions of the BIG NOTE, everything's one note. Everything, even the ponies. The note, however, is the ultimate power, but, see, the pigs don't know that, the ponies don't know that.

Hmmm, the Big Note, the universe was created by the Big Note. Hmmm, not sure about this, but wait, hold on! There has actually been scientific investigation into this by a man named Hans Jenny. Herr Jenny, a Swiss scientist, founded the scientific field known as cymantics, as opposed to semantics. And through this, he made what he perceived to be a very, very important discovery. He conducted experiments that showed that sound gave shape to matter, concluding that sound was the creative force in the universe.

So there you have it. You may have intuitively known or felt that chanting was awesome, amazing, significant, but you probably didn't know why.

Sound really is an elemental part of the universe, and perhaps the mystics of the great religions knew this.

Having said this, I do not follow the doctrine professed by Sokka Gakkai, or Nichiren Buddhism for that matter. It's the chanting I enjoy, including the recitation of the Daimoku. The Dhamma taught by Sokka Gakkai is not my cup of tea, although I know many people who have found great peace and joy through affiliation with this group.

So the next time you think disparaging thoughts about someone who chants "Nam Myoho Renge Kyo," or who recites the Pali "Namo tassa bhagavato arahato samma-sambuddhassa," because you think this person is a bit touched or affected, think about Hans Jenny. Then think about Frank Zappa and THE BIG NOTE.

17

Reaping the Benefits of Your Meditation Practice

As we move forward with our meditation practice, we will encounter obstacles. That's because Buddhism is not just meditation; it also involves living a life that avoids harming others, as well as developing wisdom. So it's worth mentioning the three-legged stool again.

Whenever I feel like my practice is losing focus, I return to this simile of the three-legged stool, something my original teacher shared with me when I first began to learn about Buddhism.

I'm sure my teacher hadn't originated this simile. The essence of this image can be found in Bhikkhu Bodhi's writings, and that of Thanissaro Bhikkhu as well (much of their work can be found on the website Access to Insight). But its simplistic beauty is worth sharing, since it had a profound impact on my practice.

Because, you see, Buddhism in North America tends to attract intellectual types, and intellectual types tend to over-think just about everything. And when it comes to Buddhism, well, their seemingly erotic fascination with esoteric passages and the nuances of the Pali language often comes off as if they were preparing a dissertation on what the jhanas symbolize within 21st Century life for the North American heterosexual male.

Sheesh. It's just Buddhism folks. Yes, it's profound; yes, it can radically change your life; yes, it can lead you to a sense of happiness unlike anything you can think of or anticipate – but it doesn't require you to stand on your head while chanting an archaic language from memorized texts in an effort to subtly dissect the mind into its components parts, if there are any component parts to begin with.

All Buddhism requires of you is to be fully aware of what you are doing right now, and understand the consequences of your actions, because out of what happens right now your future arises.

It's your movie; it wasn't written for you; you write it as you go along.

Enlightenment doesn't just magically happen because you belong to the right temple and chant all the right words with all your heart until your voice feels raspy and weak. Enlightenment is not delivered by Santa Claus because you've been a good boy or girl and followed all the precepts by rote without a shred of comprehension about what the precepts mean.

Happiness doesn't even come that way. Skip the enlightenment part – how many of us are really invested in achieving total release? Come on, anyone out there?

I want to be a good person. I want to be beneficial to others. I want to avoid actions that harm others. I want to be happy. And when I die, I want it to be without fear.

What about you?

What my practice has taught me is that over-intellectualizing hides the truth. Buddhism will reveal the truth – if you let it. But to have that happen, keep it simple; which brings me back to my teacher's simile of the three-legged stool.

There are three parts to a successful Buddhist practice: *Sila*, or virtue; *Samadhi*, or concentration; and *Panna*, or wisdom. Now think of each of these three parts as a leg on a stool. If each leg is the same length, then the seat of the stool is level and useful for comfortable sitting. When you sit on such a stool, it is stable and you feel secure; you are so comfortable you can do other things while sitting on that stool without ever thinking about whether it might tip over or you might fall off.

In other words, you are safe to be around.

Given that image, imagine what that stool might look like if all you do is read the suttas. You'll be able to quote the Buddha like some Bible-thumping idiot on a city street corner, but you won't have a clue as to why people don't like you. You'll have false wisdom, and one leg of your stool will be so much longer than the others, you will fall off.

Or if all you do is meditate. You'll have one hell of a tranquil mind, but you won't be using its potential; when people go to a dictionary and look up the word "boring," your photo will be there as the definition. And you will fall off your stool.

Or if all you do is follow the precepts. You'll be one unhappy celibate sonofabitch with spiders and cockroaches and rats all over your house, wishing you could join your friends for a beer now and then (I will spare all your delicate sensibilities about the sex part, but let me assure you, it ain't pretty). And you will fall off your stool.

Yet, I've met people who I can quickly tell either do nothing but meditate, or do nothing but read the suttas, or who do nothing but blindly follow the precepts and then criticize everyone else for not following them.

To be able to develop wisdom, you need to know the Buddha's teachings; but before you are able to really grasp the teachings, you must develop your concentration through meditation so that your mind is focused; but to effectively develop a focused mind, you must follow the precepts to develop the virtue necessary to have a mind filled with ease, knowing you haven't done something to bring about bad kamma; but to properly follow the precepts, you must have the wisdom to understand what they mean and how to apply them in your life; but to have that wisdom, you need to know what the Buddha taught and ….

See where I'm going with this? Buddhism is not linear.

Wisdom is knowing what is worthy of your mind's attention, not memorization; concentration is having the ability to use your mind to investigate the way things really are, not how you think they are; and virtue is having compassion toward others by developing the Right Actions that lead you to be harmless, not refraining from an action because someone said it is wrong.

When my teacher shared this, my brain was like – duh! This led me to attending the weekly guided meditation sessions he conducted, and to me setting aside twenty minutes every day for meditation at home. It led to me attending his weekly Dhamma class when we methodically went through the suttas and talked about what they meant in today's world. I still read the suttas over and over. And it led me to come to the dhammasala to work. I helped build a new meditation hall, helped set up and clean up before and after special occasions, and I also started hosting Dhamma study sessions at the library in the town where I lived, because the dhammasala I was attending was a 90-minute drive away and I could only go once a week, sometimes twice if I was fortunate.

That was eighteen years ago. And for the most part, that remains my practice today. Am I successful? Depends on your measure. Am I happy? You betcha, but that also depends on how you measure happiness.

I don't know if members of the industrial metal band Ministry have ever read anything by the Buddha, but the title of their fourth album – *The Mind is a Terrible Thing to Taste* – goes to the heart of Buddhist doctrine.

Virtually everything the Buddha taught, from his lessons to his son, Rahula, to his descriptions of jhana, revolve around taming the mind, bringing focus to one's mind so that discernment develops. Without discernment – the ability to tell the difference between what is skillful and unskillful, what brings good results and what brings negative results – I would continue to create kamma that keeps me bound to the endless cycle of my mundane existence. I would continue to feel restless and dissatisfied; I would continue to experience dukkha.

The third chapter of the *Dhammapada* (available in most major bookstores and online) quickly gets to the point with the opening verse to the *Citttavaga*.

> Quivering, wavering,
> hard to guard,
> to hold in check:
> the mind.

I particularly like the visual associated with this verse:

> Like a fish
> pulled from its home in the water
> and thrown on land:
> this mind flips and flaps about
> to escape Mara's sway.

By the way, Mara in Buddhist literature is thought of as both literally the devil, and symbolic of unskillful action. However, the Buddha, when speaking to other monks, used Mara symbolically, teaching the monks that hell is not a destination, but a state of mind. We go to hells that we create on our own.

Our experiences with meditation provide plenty of evidence of how difficult it can be to keep our mind focused on something as simple as breathing. We've come up with plenty of ways to describe the mind, often using various animals to portray it: the monkey mind is a common metaphor in the *Tipitika*, and meditation is frequently compared with taming an elephant. Elephants and monkeys aren't ubiquitous here in North America, which is why the notion of the "squirrel mind" is more meaningful.

However, there is a reason why taming an elephant was the dominant metaphor in the Buddha's teaching on how to control the mind. While the antics of a monkey or a squirrel are excellent at portraying how fickle the mind can be, how it jumps about from one thing to another, the metaphor of taming an elephant gets to the heart of what the mind is, or rather, what it is not.

First, let's look at verse 37 in the *Cittavaga*:

> Wandering far,
> going alone,
> bodiless,
> lying in a cave:
> the mind.
>
> Those who restrain it:
> from Mara's bonds
> they'll be freed.

The commentary explains that the cave is the body. The verse is describing the mind as being bodiless, yet it dwells within a cave. Just as the Buddha has instructed that I am not my body, I am also not my mind. Rather, I can use the mind like a tool to attain freedom.

This is why I prefer using the simile of a wild bronco to describe the mind, as it is more meaningful to my American way of thinking, and the wild bronco has the essential characteristics embodied in the elephant. When taming an elephant, the animal is often tied to a tree. Similarly, when a wild horse is to be "broken," it is frequently tied to a post within a corral. Meditation is how we restrain the mind; like the wild horse tied to the post, we "tie" our mind to breath. But the horse rebels against this restraint, pulling violently at the rope in an effort to escape.

Eventually, the horse ceases its struggling and becomes calm. But it's not over yet. The horse isn't broken yet. Because the next step is to saddle and get on the horse to ride it. And if you've ever seen a Cowboy movie, you know what happens then; the horse rebels against the saddle and rebels against having a rider on it. But if the rider is persistent, he or she eventually tames the horse and is then able to use the horse for many purposes; the horse gives in and allows itself to be directed by the rider.

And if you've seen as many Cowboy movies as I have, you know something else about the horse/rider relationship. That the rider develops a strong personal relationship with the horse, and the horse develops devotion to the rider; each becomes mutually dependent on the other.

Of course, if you grew up around horses, you know all this.

Having this type of relationship with one's mind is essential, as revealed in the last verses of the *Cittavaga*:

> Whatever an enemy might do
> to an enemy,
> or a foe to a foe,
> the ill-directed mind
> can do to you
> even worse.

> Whatever a mother, father
> or other kinsman
> might do for you,
> the well-directed mind
> can do for you
> even better.

The above are beautiful verses; almost as sublime as the opening verses to The Pairs, my favorite verses from the *Dhammapada*:

Phenomena are
preceded by the heart
ruled by the heart
made of the heart.

If you speak or act with a corrupted heart,
then suffering follows you,
as the wheel of the cart follows
the track of the ox that pulls it.

Phenomena are
preceded by the heart
ruled by the heart
made of the heart.

If you speak or act with a calm, bright heart,
then happiness follows you,
like a shadow that never leaves.

If you really want that type of happiness, the kind that never leaves you, then keep at it. You will find it.

18

Beyond Breath: Meditations on Body and Death

Even though the Buddha renounced a lay person's way of life, he remained a good father and did an outstanding job teaching his son, Rahula. We can conclude by the results that Rahula was probably an apt pupil, but that may only be because the Buddha was swift enough to re-focus his adolescent son's mind on the proper topics for contemplation, or Rahula might have been a Brahmin-style Right Said Fred.

Rahula was hot, and he knew he was hot. Or at least that's how the stories go. For example, in the notes to the *Maharahulovada Sutta* (MN 62), also known as *The Greater Discourse of Advice to Rahula*, we learn the reason why the Buddha directed his then-eighteen-year-old son to perfect the meditation technique of contemplation of the body as body.

> According to [*Majjhima Nikāya Atthakatha*] ... While Rahula was following the Buddha, he noted with admiration the physical perfection of the Master and reflected that he himself was of similar appearance, thinking: "I too am handsome like my father the Blessed One. The Buddha's form is beautiful and so too is mine." The Buddha read Rahula's thought and decided to admonish him at once, before such vain thoughts led him into greater difficulties. Hence the Buddha framed his advice in terms of contemplating the body as neither a self nor the possession of a self. (Notes are from the hardbound text, not the online text)

So dang! Rahula was a hottie twink thinking he had it goin' on, but the Buddha was wise to that nonsense and immediately re-directed his son before he started wearing Daisy Dukes and dancing on a box at a backwoods discotheque.

Contemplation of body as body is also a technique I use from time to time when I have difficultly remaining focused on my breath. It's just a different focus point and it is very effective. Besides being a necessary step in meditation – if all you do is focus on your breath, you're in a rut – when you learn to see body as just body, you come to realize that body isn't so glamorous. As my teacher once said:

"Isn't it funny that the items we attribute beauty to on our body are dead – like the outside of our skin, our teeth, our hair – but the living parts of our body – internal organs and such – we describe as gross."

The other benefit of using the body as a meditation object is that we begin to see our body as being separate from "self." There's that tricky word again, the "self." Seeing the body as it really is – I am not my body and my body is not me – keeps us in the right direction of freeing ourselves of ego. There are many places in the Buddhist canon that refer to the body as a "bag of bones," or a heap of blood and guts. It is essential we contemplate this because, bottom line, we have very little control over our bodies. The body ages without our consent, and it will cease to function whether we're ready or not.

Rahula learned well and became a significant member of the Sangha. A section of the *Theragatha* (*Verses of the Elders*) is attributed to him, where Rahula explains how the root of sensuality has been cut out of him: "Cooled am I, unbound."

I'll say so.

Contemplating our body as not ourselves also prepares us for using death as an object of meditation. Sounds morbid, I know. But when you learn to get the hang of it, meditation and contemplation on death are very stimulating.

> Fully worn out is this body,
> a nest of disease, and fragile.
> This foul mass breaks up,
> for death is the end of life.

There you go, does that cheer you up?

I've heard of people who use running like meditation, or they meditate while they run, or they get all Zen while they're running, or whatever. I don't do any of that. I just run, and try to pay attention to what my body is doing, the rhythm of my movement, the flow of my breath, even with all types of crazy shit going on inside my monkey mind. To me that's meditation: being aware. For a long time, as I've mentioned before, I used to think the goal of Buddhism and meditation was to turn off the mind's internal babble. But now I realize I don't need to try and turn it off; rather, the more I pay attention to it, the more it turns off on its own.

Thinking, at least for me, leads to self-absorption, and that hinders compassion. It's hard to be compassionate when you're obsessed with your "self," what people think about you, how you think they perceive you or think about you: It's all a mass of mental knots that stress you out. And when you cling to "self" and ego, being compassionate becomes inconvenient.

When raising your awareness of what is happening right now in this very moment all around you, opportunities present themselves. Thing is, these opportunities were there all along, the only thing different is you're living more frequently in the present moment. Now you're *seeing* them.

While on a run, I was loping along the east side of Diversey Harbor in Chicago when I see this raccoon up ahead. As I get closer, the raccoon isn't moving. Dead? No, it raises its head to look at me, but still doesn't move. I jog by, see it splayed out in the grass. It's injured.

I stop about twenty feet beyond it, look at it, see that it's very stressed. We are quite close to Lake Shore Drive; my guess is the raccoon was attempting to cross the drive, got hit, and managed to drag itself this far. It's hind legs weren't working.

Without thinking, I just started talking to the raccoon. And I was pretty blunt. Heck, the raccoon was probably going to die, its injuries mortal in nature, so I said that to the raccoon. I think it agreed with my assessment.

I called animal control because I didn't want anyone else messing with the animal. People can be assholes. The guy at animal control took my information and said he would call someone from the wildlife division. I told the raccoon; maybe they could help you, I said.

The raccoon started to drag itself across the sidewalk toward the harbor. It was going to deliberately throw itself into the harbor. Was I about to witness a raccoon suicide?

"You know the end is near, don't you," I said to it. "It's alright, we all have to go someday. Wish I could help you."

I spoke quietly, gently. It dragged itself a little more, then paused at the edge of the cement wall. That's when I took a photo. It paused for a moment, heaving from the exertion, then pulled itself over and plunged into the harbor.

I peered over the edge, saw it paddle with its front legs, the rear legs still useless.

"I bet that cold water feels good, but if you take off, the wildlife people won't find you and fix you."

It looked up at me as it paddled along the edge. "Screw the wildlife people, I don't need them," it said.

Oh, wait, it didn't say anything. Raccoons can't talk. It just looked up at me and swam away.

I have no idea what happened to that raccoon. My presumption is the injuries were fatal. I just hope that in its last moments, my presence brought it a little comfort, reduced its stress just a tad as it faced the end. Because, you know, when I die, I hope someone will be there with me too.

And now when I run by that spot, I put my palms together and bow my head in respect for the raccoon who gave me a lesson on both life and death.

Most of us think we fully understand that we will die one day, or that others in our lives will die. But that's not contemplating death, that's not being fully aware of death. That's something we avoid thinking about. And the reason we avoid thinking about it is we tend to identify our bodies as being who we are, rather than seeing the body for what it really is.

Contemplating death from time to time prepared me for my mother's death. It helped in the last months when her dementia left her unable to distinguish her body from a chair she'd be sitting in. We commonly say things like, "She's not there anymore," when describing someone with dementia, and it's true. Yet we continue to say things like, "My father is here," simply because the body remains alive. My mother's body continued to live well past the time "she" had ceased. And when her body did give in, my reaction was peaceful and even elated because I knew then her suffering was over.

In fact, I had the opportunity to meditate over her body. One of my sisters called me to say that mom was in the hospital and it looked like it was the end. I had about a three-hour drive to get there and by the time I arrived, she was dead. My sisters and I gathered around the body in the hospital room, chatted a bit, and when they left the room I stayed behind.

Standing there, my hands held in front of me, I began to concentrate on my breath. My mind emptied, and I gazed upon the corpse fully aware that that was not my mother, it was just a body, my mother was gone, she was free of suffering. I felt sorrow, but I felt relieved as well.

I firmly believe that through contemplating death occasionally during meditation, or even during momentary breaks throughout the day, prepared me for when I had a stroke, and a year later, a heart attack. I incorporated these events into my meditation, using them to strengthen my understanding of how my body is not me, and I am not my body, and in the process, I reached a new understanding of what mindfulness truly entails.

I had a conception of what it meant, what being mindful was all about. And in that notion was a root connected to raw awareness. But I began to realize I had been looking beyond that raw awareness and seeking something else that I thought was mindfulness.

My stroke changed that.

It was a minor stroke, one caused by a clot in the vision center of my brain. It affected my peripheral vision on my left side in both eyes. Everything else – motor skills, speech, cognitive abilities, taste, smell – remain unaffected. To give you an idea, when I'm sitting in the passenger seat of a car, I can see just fine straight ahead. And I have normal peripheral vision to the right. But my vision ends at the center console. I can't see the driver at all unless I turn my head.

Needless to say, I bump into doorways on the left side frequently because I can't see the left side of the door jamb. People or other moving objects coming up from behind me and passing on the left startle me because I don't see them until they've already passed and are almost in front of me. And unless I look directly at what I am reaching for, I may misjudge and fail to grasp it if it's on my left.

This presented some rather harsh and immediate lessons about mindfulness. It changed the way I think about mindfulness. It's not this overall gestalt that I used to think it as; rather it's very specific. Mindfulness doesn't just mean being aware of the world around me any longer. It means being aware of what I am doing right now in this world around me, and that means just a small part of this world around me, not this big expansive world that I had been thinking about.

My moment of realization came when I was being discharged from the hospital. I was elated I was finally getting out. I'd spent four days there waiting for tests to be completed. As I was gathering my belongings, I reached to my left for a Styrofoam cup of ice water I knew was there. But instead of grasping the cup, I closed my hand too soon, puncturing my thumb through the side of the Styrofoam and spilling water onto the table.

It was then I realized what being mindful really meant, what was really required of me. And it also made me aware of how I had taken for granted my awareness and my "mindfulness." No longer could I be casual about even the simplest thing such as reaching for a cup of water. No longer could I be automatic while doing something as simple as walking through a doorway. When dining out, I must be extra sensitive to a server coming in from my left, or a glass or utensil on my left. And when I cross the street from now on, my life depends on my mindfulness more than it ever has before.

Believe me, if given a choice I would not want to reach such an understanding by having a stroke. But I did have one. That can't be changed. And now I'm ready for a new day.

19

Right and Wrong and the Pitfalls of Relativism

BUDDHISM, IN PART, IS ABOUT ASKING QUESTIONS to determine how things really are. But to truly see the truth, you have to ask the right questions. And the question on my mind at the moment is whether Honey Boo Boo is foreshadowing the decline of civilization.

Homo say what? Honey Boo Boo?

Come to the light, children, there is still hope for you.

I have never watched Honey Boo Boo, nor many of the other television shows of this genre I like to call fake reality TV. I did watch an online trailer for the show prior to its indecorous debut and that was enough. I wanted to cleanse my eyes with Comet after that. I saw enough, however, to know instantly that civilization was perched upon a perilous precipice, over which it could tumble into oblivion at any moment.

We, in a collective sense, have only ourselves to blame for this type of programming dreck. And to add insult to injury, the folks in TV-land have created elaborate methods to convince you that the programming available is, in fact, high quality backed by tons of creative minds.

I mean, they hand out awards for this stuff, so it has to be legit!

It's all a diversion designed to lull you into a false sense of happiness so that you will more readily accept the commercial content that batters your psyche with often better production quality than the programs it sponsors. Its intent is to stupify you in a manner Bob Dylan eloquently described in his song, "It's Alright Ma (I'm Only Bleeding)".

The song describes how advertising tricks you into thinking that everything is about you, for you, that you can accomplish impossible things, even win something like the lottery, and this deception redirects our thoughts and actions toward attaining these fantasies. But the real result is life passes us by because we weren't paying attention.

This is precisely why the Buddha advised a young fellow named Sigala to avoid theatrical shows.

Patience my pretties. I think a reason why many practitioners do not read Dhamma is quite similar as to why other folk do not read the Bible or whatever holy book guides their religion, the reason being that the language in these texts is archaic and not easily understood. For that reason, it can be easily viewed as irrelevant to today's culture.

It also means the message in these texts can be easily distorted by "teachers" interested only in feeding their rapacious egos.

For example, in the *Sigalovada Sutta*, the Buddha includes "watching theatrical shows" as an item in a list of activities that lead to the loss of wealth. And then he enumerates the reasons why and how watching theatrical shows results in this:

> here are, young householder, these six evil consequences in frequenting theatrical shows. He is ever thinking:
>
> (i) where is there dancing?
> (ii) where is there singing?
> (iii) where is there music?
> (iv) where is there recitation?
> (v) where is there playing with cymbals?
> (vi) where is there pot-blowing?

Pot-blowing? What the hell is that? And what's wrong with singing and dancing?

This is what I'm talking about. People look at this and think that Buddhism is irrelevant in today's world. The problem, however, is not that Buddhism lacks relevance; the problem is the question – we aren't asking the right questions.

No, there is nothing wrong with singing, or dancing, or even pot-blowing, provided we don't get too carried away. Remember the Buddha described his path as the Middle Way. He tried the extremes and found them lacking. The path to spiritual bliss is neither followed by extreme pleasure nor by extreme deprivation. And while we follow the way in the middle, we must be honest in evaluating our emotions.

Remember what the First Noble Truth is? For many people, life is more than just unsatisfactory, it can really suck, and too many of us queer folk know this all too well. But for most people, life is how Henry David Thoreau described it when he said, "Most men lead lives of quiet desperation and go to the grave with the song still in them."

Believe it or not, shows like Honey Boo Boo are tapping into a collective sense of dismay and dissatisfaction that permeate our lives. It presents an opportunity, albeit a false one, for us to watch someone else's life self-destruct and gives us a sense that things can't be all that bad, "thank god I'm not in Honey Boo Boo's family!"

But like the theatrical shows the Buddha warned Sigala about, this is a distraction that keeps us in our self-dug hole of dissatisfaction. Shows like Honey Boo Boo aren't designed to uplift us, to inspire us; they're designed to keep us in a rut of meaningless existence, to set us up for the next string of commercials that will entice us to spend money on goods and services we don't need and which, if we took just a few seconds to think about it, we don't want.

There are a lot of unhappy people in the world. We can't help them all. But are you at least trying to help a few of them?

Start by helping yourself first. Begin by learning how to ask the right questions. Ponder, for example, what is right and what is wrong?

Within Buddhist circles, you eventually hear someone say there is no right and wrong, that these terms merely represent a dualistic form of thinking that creates imaginary categories that are empty.

On one level, I believe that to be true. On another level, I believe such talk is total nonsense. And it is this type of Wrong Thinking that in my view leads others to conclude that Buddhism is amoral.

There is right and wrong in Buddhism. In fact, the Buddha made a list to show us that there is right and wrong. He called this list The Noble Eightfold Path. Because in order to have Right View, you must abandon Wrong View; if you want to develop Right Intention, you must abandon Wrong Intention; if you want to develop Right Speech, you must abandon Wrong Speech; to develop Right Action, you must abandon Wrong Action; to engage in Right Livelihood, you must abandon Wrong Livelihood; to develop Right Effort, you must abandon Wrong Effort; to develop Right Mindfulness, you must avoid Wrong Mindfulness; and to achieve Right Concentration, you must abandon Wrong Concentration.

That's the Buddha's rap, folks – there is Right and Wrong.

These items in The Noble Eightfold Path are further categorized by the Buddha pertaining to how an item in the path relates to one of the three basic elements of the Buddhist practice: Panna, or wisdom; Samadhi, or concentration; and Sila, or virtue. That's right! Virtue is a key element of the Buddhist practice. It's what following the Five Precepts is all about – developing virtue!

Where the confusion arises is in the way we Westerners tend to view these terms right and wrong. While these terms are synonymous with "correct" and "incorrect," when speaking about human behavior, these terms are generally imbued with moralistic tones that derive from our shared monotheistic background. Something is morally right or morally wrong because an action is considered morally right by the assertion it is a directive from a higher power or it pleases a higher power, and if an action is contrary to that higher power's directive or displeases that higher power, then that action is deemed morally wrong.

But that's not the way these terms work in Buddhism. Whether an action or other phenomenon can be consider "right" or "wrong" is not determined by a third-party entity, but rather by the results created by that phenomenon.

The phenomenon is "right" when it results in the alleviating one's own suffering, the suffering of others, or one's own suffering and the suffering of others. The phenomenon is wrong when it results in increased suffering for self, increased suffering for others, or increased suffering for both self and others. And yes, the Buddha also spoke of morally neutral actions, actions that neither alleviate nor cause suffering for self or others.

Results are not always just immediate. We can engage in actions that bring us the immediate result of diminishing our own suffering. But actions set in motion many things, and there may be later results that lead to greater suffering. So while an action may look "right" in the short term, that same action may later be revealed to be quite wrong.

It's not that difficult to grasp. The Buddha taught his son Rahula this when the boy was just seven years old. But again and again, discussions about morality veer way off into the very highest limbs and the remotest leaves of the tallest simsapa trees.

Now granted, it is important for us to understand why a wrong action is a wrong action. It's important to understand why it's wrong so that we can stop committing that action. But not understanding why something is wrong should never hinder us from stopping that action. And even if I never fully understand why something is wrong, if I'm convinced it is by other reasons, then I am doing something very skillful by ceasing that action. I will get good results regardless of whether I understand why a former action was wrong. And for many people, that's good enough.

While Buddhism is pretty simple, it is also quite subtle. While a wrong action will often bring immediate or near-term bad results, the Buddha taught a theory of kamma that diverged significantly from the dominate theory in India at the time. Despite the fact we may commit a wrong act in the present, we have the opportunity to diminish its continual negative influence over time through engaging in Right Action.

While the Buddha, for example, told soldiers that by developing proper mental attitudes during battle would reduce the kammic impact of their actions – killing people – he was quite clear that the soldiers would never escape those kammic consequences. Consider the simile of the salt crystal.

In this story, the Buddha asks a group of monks: if one puts a tablespoon of salt into a glass of water, will that change the water's taste? The monks reply of course it will. The water will become undrinkable, say the monks.

The Buddha then asks if you put a tablespoon of salt into the Ganges, will you be able to taste the salt? The monks reply, no, because there is so much water in the Ganges the salt will be diluted and undetectable.

With the simile of the salt crystal, the Buddha explains if we're lucky enough and have enough time, we can correct and change future outcomes for previous bad acts. He says this also to Angulimala (more on him in Chapter 21) when he tells the former robber and murderer to quit his whining: by suffering now Angulimala can avoid the torment of eons in a hell realm.

This is why I often say there is no moral right to do anything, but there are consequences for everything. We may feel that we "deserve" to react to someone or something in a particular way, and we may opt to follow on our impulse or belief. As Clint Eastwood classically said in *The Unforgiven*, "Deserves got nothing to do with it."

But no matter how we rationalize our action later, no matter how vehemently we seek to justify our action, our action creates consequences, both short- and long-term. We could, for example, feel great at the moment, but later feel remorse and guilt for years. Do what you will, but you shall reap what you sow. You are where you are because you went there.

We'll explore this more closely in the chapter on Kamma. In preparation, here's a tool to assist you in asking the right questions: The Four Right Efforts.

Every day is an opportunity to practice the Dhamma with greater skill than the previous day. And every day holds the potential of being our last. January 1 is no more special a day in this regard then March 12, or August 7. Every day is an opportunity for us to better ourselves and to be of greater service to others. Every day is a chance to wipe away a bit more of the film of delusion that covers our eyes and sedates our mind, to rattle our helter skelter actions and bring them out of the self-induced soporific trance of false comfort, to open our eyes and see things for how they really are, not what we wish them to be.

That takes effort – four of them to be precise. And to correctly apply these four efforts, we need to be well-grounded in the present moment.

There are many sayings that reflect to a degree the importance of remaining focused on the present. There is "One day at a time," perhaps the most common and very effective at reminding us that we shouldn't dwell too much on the future. But this axiom can be used for selfish ends; for some it is a more palatable form of "eat, drink and be merry for tomorrow you may die," because it can make us sound like we're being more responsible. It would be something like spending your life in a gay disco, dancing away the days with all the hot go-go boys, waiting for that moment at the end of the night when all the studly men and boys take off their shirts.

There is *carpe diem*, or "seize the day," which is a much more aggressive way of reminding us that today may well be our last, so we ought to get as much out of it as we can. This does, however, allow hedonism to run amok in our life because this saying tends to give permission for unrestrained indulgence in sensual pleasure. It would be like spending your life in a gay sauna where you aren't so much seizing the day, but turgid appendages of flesh.

This adage gets closer to the heart of the matter: "If yesterday is a canceled check, today is cash, and tomorrow a promissory note, go with the cash and spend it today." But even this allows for personal indulgence in empty spending purely for immediate gratification. It's like throwing away all your credit cards and only using cash, but you're still acquiring objects that have no real value and bring you no closer to true happiness as there will always be some new item you don't and must have.

No, living in the present moment is simpler than that, and yet it's more difficult to achieve. In the *Theranama Sutta*, we hear about a solitary monk named Thera who brags about the virtue of living alone. When the Buddha hears about this, he tells Thera that there is his (Thera's) way of "being alone," but there is a better way.

> And how is living alone perfected in its details? There is the case where whatever is past is abandoned, whatever is future is relinquished, and any passion and desire with regard to states of being attained in the present is well subdued. That is how living alone is perfected in its details.

The Buddha relays this message in a slightly different form in the *Bhaddekaratta Sutta* as well.

> You shouldn't chase after the past
> or place expectations on the future.
> What is past
> is left behind.
> The future
> is as yet unreached.
> Whatever quality is present
> you clearly see right there,
> right there.
> Not taken in,
> unshaken,

that's how you develop the heart.
Ardently doing
what should be done today,
for – who knows? – tomorrow
death.
There is no bargaining
with Mortality and his mighty horde.

Whoever lives thus ardently,
relentlessly
both day and night,
has truly had an auspicious day:
so says the Peaceful Sage.

So there it is. Living in the present moment means avoid dwelling in the past because the past is gone. It also means that we recognize that where we are right now is because of what happened in the past. The past is important because it brings us to the here and now, but to dwell on the past cripples us.

Pining for the future, or even just thinking about the future, is of no use as well because the future is not here. But recognizing that our future is built upon our present actions is very important. It is only by behaving skillfully in the present can we erase the kamma we created in the past and build a happier future for ourselves.

To help us accomplish this, the Buddha gave us the Four Right Efforts. While I've previously mentioned these, they bear repeating. They are:

1. To prevent unskillful qualities from arising
2. To denourish and remove unskillful qualities already present
3. To strengthen and further develop skillful qualities already present
4. To nurture and develop skillful qualities not present so they may arise

There are bad actions that we already don't do, and that's good. But we need to make sure that these bad actions never manifest themselves. For example, if we've never intentionally killed anyone, it's a good idea to make sure we don't in the future.

No one is a saint, so there are negative actions we engage in that we need to identify and remove. If we smoke, it would be wise to stop smoking. This example oversimplifies matters, so don't be beguiled by its apparent simplicity. We all exhibit many subtle negative behaviors that we may not immediately recognize. When we do, we need to strive to remove them.

We all have good qualities. We don't want to lose them, so we need to strengthen them, just as we would strengthen our body through exercise. If we don't, we may lose these good qualities, and that would be a bad thing.

Then there are the qualities that we wish to have, that we want to develop. Qualities that we admire in others and wish to emulate. We must work at developing these qualities, because they don't spontaneously arise. We cannot become more compassionate toward others unless we practice compassion daily. We won't become more empathetic unless we seek to understand others around us. Our concentration during meditation will not improve unless we work at mindfulness in everything we do and say.

20

The Elements of Kamma

I WAS HAVING DINNER ONE EVENING with a friend who asked me about kamma, which led to me explaining that kamma was often misrepresented even by those who call themselves Buddhist. People tend to think of kamma as the result of an action. For example, "Don't do that, it will bring you bad karma."

I tend to use the Pali term kamma rather than the Sanskrit term karma because my Buddhist education is grounded in the Thai Forest Tradition. Either term will work, however.

Anyway, I told my friend that kamma isn't created by the action, but rather the intention behind the action. One creates kamma via his or her intentions.

He then asked me about light and dark kamma, and that's when I had to admit ignorance. I had an idea of how to explain bright and dark kamma, but I didn't want to misstate something. So I told my friend I would study the matter first.

That sent me on my first in-depth analysis of kamma and all that it entails. And it's a lot. It's probably one of the most well-known Buddhist concepts, and yet, it's also perhaps the most misunderstood and misrepresented.

If you're going to practice Buddhism, you're going to need a working understanding of Kamma. And it's going to make your head swim at times.

Breathe in. Breathe out.

The best expression of what bright and dark kamma is can be found in the *Anguttara Nikāya*. The particular passage can be found in Thanissaro Bhikkhu's "Beyond Coping" in the section on Heedfulness, which you can find on the website Access to Insight.

And while not dealing specifically with the concepts of bright and dark kamma, the story of Angulimala also provides some excellent insights into the workings of kamma.

In the Anguttara Nikāya, the Buddha lays out four types of kamma:

> There is kamma that is dark with dark result; kamma that is bright with bright result; kamma that is dark and bright with dark and bright result; and kamma that is neither dark nor bright with neither dark nor bright result, leading to the ending of kamma.

As the Buddha explains each of these four types of kamma, it's important to note the language used.

"And what is kamma that is dark with dark result? There is the case where a certain person fabricates an injurious bodily fabrication..." The Buddha uses the phrase, "a certain person fabricates ..." The concept of fabrications is pretty important in Buddhism; trouble is most people have the wrong idea of what it means.

Many people think that when something is a "fabrication," it means that object or construct is not real, that it doesn't exist at all. In my view, that's not at all what the Buddha means when he talks about fabrications. On one level, fabrications are not real in and of themselves, but the object or event to which we attach the fabrication is real.

In the Buddhist sense, a fabrication is merely a mental construct created by our mind to give some object or event a characteristic that we wrongly view as permanent. Recall the line Juliet speaks when thinking of Romeo's family name: "What's in a name? That which we call a rose by any other name would smell as sweet."

A rose is a rose no matter what we call it. As a collection of matter, a rose simply is. The name "rose" is the mental fabrication we create to ascribe to a plant that has certain physical characteristics. Go to a different country where a different language is spoken and the mental construct has a different pronunciation, but the rose is still a rose.

When the Buddha describes kamma, it is connected with the mental fabrication associated with the intent to commit an act of either speech, body, or mind. So in the case of dark kamma, that fabrication begins with wrong intent, with an intent to cause harm. The consequences that manifest after an intention of dark kamma are the results of kamma, the fruits of kamma, not the kamma itself. Bright kamma, by contrast, begins with a fabrication that causes no harm. Hence, the fruits of bright kamma are pleasant.

We often get confused when we seem to get mixed results from our actions because we think we have a good intention. This is what the Buddha refers to as kamma that is both bright and dark. As Thanissaro Bhikkhu explains here, we may think we have good intentions, but if we really examine our intentions, they are often unclear and confused; hence the outcomes of our actions bring us confusing or mixed results.

This happens a lot in interpersonal relationships, particularly among those of us in the LGBTQ community.

Remember the film *The Broken Hearts Club* and how Dennis befriended the cute newbie Kevin (oh god, Kevin was such a darling!)? Dennis clearly had the hots for Kevin, but he wanted to appear more virtuous than the callous Cole, so Dennis concocts this idea that Kevin needs a true friend when Dennis' real intention is to get Kevin in bed.

All of Dennis' friends see this for how it really is, but Dennis chooses to believe in his false intention. While the outcome is not completely messed up, the results definitely are mixed.

Most of our lives are filled with this combination of bright and dark kamma because for most of us, we really don't understand our real intentions, either because we willfully ignore them or because we just never really took a close look at our actions and the motivations behind them.

This is why we meditate. To stop the chatter in our minds so that we can see the truth behind all our thoughts, words and deeds.

Angulimala, a legendary thief and murderer, ran into this problem even after the Buddha accepted him into the Sangha.

At first, Angulimala couldn't get anyone to offer him food during his alms rounds because he remained feared and despised for all of his past murderous actions. Even after the Buddha set up an act of truth to show others Angulimala's new noble birth and he became accepted by more villagers, there remained a group who refused to believe that Angulimala was nothing more than a murderous monster.

Whenever he went for alms, these holdouts threw rocks and sticks at him. One time he comes to the Buddha, his head bleeding, to show the Buddha what had happened. The Buddha tells Angulimala to buck up and endure this because he is lucky to be suffering this torment now as the continuing fruits of his past actions rather than to suffer those consequences by spending eons in a hell realm.

Remember the simile of the salt crystal mentioned in an earlier chapter?

The final type of kamma is what the Buddha describes as being neither dark nor bright. This is when we abandon all kamma and we are free of any intention other than to liberate ourselves from the cycle of birth and death. I haven't a clue as to what that must be like. My days are still mixed with brightness and darkness, a muddle of intentions that I am barely able to discern.

What complicates things even more is that our own kamma is also mixed up with the kamma of our relatives.

Remember Tiger Woods? Sure, he's pretty well known. And I'm sure you remember the mess he created with his extra-marital affairs.

But do you remember Joseph Stack? Short version is he flew a plane into a corporate building in Austin, Texas in a suicide attack back in 2010.

Remember these guys for the moment.

After every sitting meditation session, I recite two things: the Loving Kindness chant and the Five Recollections. Within the Five Recollections is this line:

> I am the owner of my kamma, born of my kamma, related to my kamma, abide supported in my kamma – whatever kamma I do, skillful or unskillful, to that I fall heir.

The key element to this particular verse for the purpose of this passage is the phrase, "I am ... related to my kamma ..."

When I first heard this, I asked my teacher what it meant. He said it literally means that the people you are related to are part of your kamma. The parents I had were not an accident, nor was it "fate" or random that I have the siblings that I do. And all the people I've had other types of relations with – friendly, professional, intimate, antagonistic – are connected to my kamma.

These people are in my life because of past actions. If you're one to believe in the concept of rebirth, then these people are in our lives because of past actions either in this present life or from a previous life. If you're like me, who doesn't think believing in rebirth is critical to being Buddhist, then it's the connections created since my birth and the actions I've taken.

And how I manage these relationships determines whether I am abandoning kamma or creating more.

Holy shit, I thought. That is some heavy duty stuff. I was stunned with the concept. Because if these people are in my life because of past actions, then how I deal with them right now determines my future kamma and my future life!

Hold on to that thought for a moment.

Joseph Stack was a troubled man; that is not too difficult for anyone to see. His despair must have been profound. Yet, when you read his manifesto (it's easily found via the Google), it becomes very clear that he accepted no personal responsibility for his actions.

He quite plainly took significant time to justify in his mind what he intended to do (remember, kamma is based on intent):

> I would only hope that by striking a nerve that stimulates the inevitable double standard, knee-jerk government reaction that results in more stupid draconian restrictions people wake up and begin to see the pompous political thugs and their mindless minions for what they are. Sadly, though I spent my entire life trying to believe it wasn't so, but violence not only is the answer, it is the only answer.

What a desperate and deluded mind to reach such an ominous conclusion. And we learned that it wasn't just the people in that building in Austin who were being targeted by his delusion.

Prior to his fateful flight, the night before, he had a terrible argument with his wife, who fled with their daughter to spend the night elsewhere. Thank goodness for that. For the next day, Stack set fire to his home before he fled to attempt mass murder.

Now think about that phrase, "I am … related to my kamma …" Think of all the people Stack has pulled into his kammic universe.

Now let us consider Tiger Woods. Did you watch his statement when he made it following that debacle over the affairs? I did, and while listening to him speak, even before he began talking about his Buddhist faith, I recalled the Buddha's teaching to his son Rahula.

> Rahula, it's like a royal elephant: immense, pedigreed, accustomed to battles, its tusks like chariot poles. Having gone into battle, it uses its forefeet and hindfeet, its forequarters and hindquarters, its head and ears and tusks and tail, but keeps protecting its trunk. The elephant trainer notices that and thinks, "This royal elephant has not given up its life to the king." But when the royal elephant … having gone into battle, uses its forefeet and hindfeet, its forequarters and hindquarters, its head and ears and tusks and tail and his trunk, the trainer notices that and thinks, "This royal elephant has given up its life to the king. There is nothing it will not do."
>
> In the same way, Rahula, when anyone feels no shame in telling a deliberate lie, there is no evil, I tell you, he will not do. Thus, Rahula, you should train yourself, "I will not tell a deliberate lie even in jest."

While I listened to Woods speak, I saw a royal elephant. Granted, he completely messed things up with his wife and children, but you could tell he recognized that. He took complete and unequivocal responsibility for his own actions. He owned them.

And he admitted that simply saying he was sorry wouldn't change anything. He had to change. And by recognizing this, he has the opportunity in this life to diminish the kamma he has created.

Just as the chapter is titled, these are just the basic elements of kamma. I hope it will get you started with a working idea of the concept as you further investigate Buddhist doctrine. And I certainly encourage you to investigate further.

One way to further this investigation is to read the *Maha-kammavibhanga*

Sutta (MN 136). It's a delightful read, because the message within this sutta is particularly applicable to the gay community.

There are really two messages being delivered by the Buddha in this sutta: one is regarding the trap of dogma, and the other is that kamma operates in such a complex manner that even the well-learned student of Buddhism can have difficulty understanding it.

Kamma is one of those Buddhist paradoxes: the concept is very simple – when this is, that is – but how kamma operates is extraordinarily arcane.

For example, why is it that person A, who's been a slut all his life and has the emotional warmth of a lizard is still alive and healthy, while person B – who everyone recognizes is the sweetest guy around, who has been a community activist most of his life, and who has been loyal to his partner – dies of AIDS at a young age?

Imagine this being taken a step further, however, because in the *Mahakammavibhanga Sutta*, the Buddha offers the scenario of someone having the ability, through meditation, to see what happens to these people after they die.

Suppose you were able to discern that a violently homophobic man who brutally murders a gay man winds up reborn as an animal after death? What might you generalize from this?

The Buddha explains with examples, such as of a learned monk who, during meditation, reaches a state of concentration when he "sees" what happens after death to someone who has committed transgressions: that person goes to hell.

From that "insight," a very rigid conclusion is reached that all people who commit transgressions are destined for hell. Rather than true insight, this point of view becomes trapped in a narrow dogma.

How many of us are trapped in dogma? Such rigid dogma is all over the place within the gay community when you think about it. We even have terms to identify these dogmas and place people in their respective "camps."

There are the "sex-positive" queers; the "circuit boys;" the "assimilation-ists." There are those who believe that monogamy and nesting is the only responsible way to express our sexuality, and anyone who has multiple partners is irresponsible. And there are others who believe that having multiple partners unencumbered by the heterosexist norm of marriage is the only true way to express our homosexuality.

Does this sound like anyone you know?

The Buddha in his great teaching on kamma explains that such a rigid interpretation of kamma is false. That, in fact, there are people who commit transgressions during life and who reach heavenly states after death; conversely, there are people who live virtuous lives who at times find themselves in hell.

The Buddha's point is that kamma is a complex interaction of many events, intentions and actions, and the results of kamma develop in different ways for different people. Add to that the fact that we cannot know everything about a person's life experiences, so how can we possibly know what type of kamma he or she is developing?

That, however, hasn't stopped us from talking like we do know someone else's kamma, or that we do know how kamma functions for us in light of the precepts – particularly the Third and Fifth precepts.

For example, a gay man who is in an open relationship mutually agreed-upon with his partner may believe that his kamma is "good" because he finds his other sex partners at bars or circuit events. And this same person may have a dim view of someone who seeks partners in a bathhouse. Yet, the guy in the bathhouse may completely abstain from all drugs and alcohol and practices safe-sex only.

What of the closeted gay married to a woman? He is the guy who has long ago stopped having sex with his wife, but continues to furtively masturbate to gay porn. He's remained faithful to his wife, hasn't he? The Third Precept has been kept, right?

And yet he is miserable. Is that his kamma?

What can get overlooked in discussions like these is that the men I previously described are equally "trapped" by the fetters of their sensual desires. They are all accumulating kamma, a kamma that will play a deterministic role in their futures.

The Buddha did not teach that following his path meant the accumulation of kamma; rather, he teaches that liberation from suffering is accomplished through the diminishment of kamma.

We all want to understand the nature of kamma. But more and more I am realizing that all I can really discern is whether the actions, thoughts and words I am involved in during the here and now are paving the way for future benefit, the future diminishment of kamma. And I must be prepared for unexpected results that may be the fruition of kamma that might have a source I cannot identify. Which is why I find refuge in the *Lonaphala Sutta* (AN 3.99), *The Salt Crystal*.

Gay or lesbian, I believe we can be sexual beings and live a moral life; the Buddha's teachings not only allow for this, but provide very useful guidance on this. But of the three ailments all of us humans suffer from – greed, hatred, and delusion – the ailment of delusion is the most difficult to deal with because it can be the most difficult to identify within ourselves.

When we see our delusions for what they are, the experience is not just liberating. It is transformative.

21

Buddhism for the modern homosexual and gender identity variant

BUDDHISM HAS A LONG TRADITION TOWARD CONFORMITY, and that's not a healthy tradition for today's LGBTQ person. So while I firmly believe Buddhism offers the best way of life for gay and non-binary people, it remains fraught with oppressive and discriminatory dogma.

This goes way back in the Buddhist canon and can be found in even relatively recent commentaries. There's even a story of the Buddha ousting a monk from the Sangha because of the monk's lewd and lascivious conduct with other men. This story has been used by others as an example to justify an anti-gay stance within Buddhism. It also is used to suggest that men who behave like women are inherently to be distrusted.

More thoughtful interpretations of the story suggest the Buddha's decision to oust the monk was based on the negative publicity the monk's behavior was creating within the nearby community, upon which the entire Sangha was dependent. It didn't matter that the monk desired sex with many men. The problem was he desired sex at all. Monks are supposed to be celibate.

But it's a story. Did it even really happen? Because increasingly, scholars are determining that most of what is considered the Buddha's teachings, or "what he said," were written long after the Buddha's death with little to no evidence he ever said any of it at all.

Pick up the book *Greek Buddha* by Christopher I. Beckwith, who suggests the only item we can clearly attribute to the Buddha – or at least to the time period when the Buddha was alive – is The Four Noble Truths. We can't even be certain if we can directly attribute the Noble Eightfold Path to the Buddha as it might have been created long after his death.

Which means any story attributed to the Buddha regarding homosexuality or gender-nonconforming people is of dubious origin.

This is why reading and absorbing as much Dhamma as possible, as well as developing a consistent meditation practice, is so important. Remaining vigorous in these efforts will eventually lead us to understanding and ultimate wisdom.

However, the path for us lay practitioners is fraught with peril – peril from our own deluded minds that can lead us to inappropriate, or unskillful, conclusions, as well as from allegedly wise and reliable teachers who misinform us, either unintentionally through their own unskillful ignorance, or intentionally through their own massive egos deluded by Wrong View.

Let's first get the easy parts done.

In and of itself, being homosexual is neutral: It is neither right nor wrong. The same is true for being gender nonconforming, or trans, or bisexual. Anyone who identifies with any of these monikers knows it is something well beyond any ability to freely choose.

In and of itself, at its basest level, sexual activity of any type is neutral: It is neither right nor wrong. And I really mean that – sex, in and of itself, is neutral.

I can already hear some of you object. "Clearly, you don't mean sex between and adult and child? Clearly you can't mean sex with animals?"

Oh dear, take a deep breath. Breathe in, breathe out.

Of course I don't mean that an adult engaging in sex with a child is a morally neutral act. Would you listen to yourself? I am purely talking about mechanics here. Sticking a penis into a vagina cannot claim higher moral ground than sticking a penis into a mouth or rectum. Or even an inanimate object such as a FleshJack or a blowup doll. Two men having sex does not occupy a lower moral plane than sex between a man and woman.

And especially, missionary-style sex can claim no higher moral ground than being a sub wearing a puppy mask with a puppy tail butt plug being led around with a leash.

Sex is sex, and contains no inherent value of its own.

But who we have sex with, and how many, or how often, frequently becomes a matter that many people think they can not only opine on, but regulate as well. People do seem to have this idea they can judge others by the type of sex they have or whether there's one or many partners, or whether the partner is the same sex.

For example, I've encountered many gay people who sneer at the idea of an older man partnering with a younger man, especially if the dynamic of Daddy/Son role-play is added to the mix. And ironically, many of these same condescending people willingly place themselves into more traditional, monogamous relationships filled with deceit, manipulation, and distrust, and which ultimately either become destructive – perhaps even violent – or end in breakup.

But, hey, "we're a normal relationship. The fact you guys have to wear leather is weird."

Now, now, honey. We don't "have" to wear leather. We choose to.

So let's examine some portions of the canon to see how they might relate to sex in general, and homosexual sex in particular.

I ran into a discussion on my Facebook page years ago that left me clueless as to a response. And it was about sex for goodness sake! Me clueless and unable to give a response about sex? I may have to give my toaster back! (you may only get that last reference if you were a diligent viewer of Ellen DeGeneres' ill-fated TV series, you know, before she became the talk-show goddess that she is today)

Ellen, can you hear me? Can you feel me near you? Ellen, can you feel me? Can I help to cheer you? Ooo-oo-oo, Ellen, Ellen, Ellen.

OK, enough references to 1960s rock operas (but seriously, don't you think Tommy was just a tad gay?)

Someone had posited that having multiple sex partners was fine and within the intention of the Third Precept as long as everything was consensual. Why would there be a preference inferred within the Third Precept for monogamy over polygamy or polyamory?

And I have to say that when this question was asked, I had no easy response. Instead, I asked more questions. And one of the questions I asked was whether this person had read any of the Buddhist literature, such as the Pali canon.

His reply was he had not.

Now, the fact that he hadn't read any of the Pali canon did not on its own render his opinion worthless. Not at all.

His position that as long as one was behaving through proper social norms, having multiple sex partners would be within the intent of the Third Precept; just don't be possessive of another and make sure that it's consensual.

Sounds all very reasonable. Perhaps beguiling? Because at the time, and we're talking more than a decade ago, I couldn't be sure.

I had to agree that if one remained uncommitted, multiple sexual partners under the rubric of everything being consensual was probably within the intent of the Third Precept. But was such activity skillful?

That was what was troubling me. Because my gut said no, it is not skillful, and it holds tremendous potential for future pain, suffering, anguish, misunderstanding, mistrust, and – not to forget – some nasty little diseases that may crop up.

But was I confusing "risk" for "skillfulness?"

Having said that, I needed something to back me up, to support my conclusion. Because sometimes the trouble with Buddhism is there are a lot of people who will identify as Buddhist who really don't know much about what the Buddha taught. And it just seemed prudent to me that if you are going to identify as Buddhist, it would be wise to know something about the subject before deciding what is considered skillful Buddhist behavior.

I'm just sayin'.

And finally, I found my response. All it took was me picking up my copy of the *Majjhima Nikāya*.

And what I found was the *Ratthapala Sutta*! Oh yeah, this guy Ratthapala had it goin' on! While I'm sure there are other suttas that will address this question more specifically, I found Ratthapala's discussion on the four teachings of the Buddha that attracted him to Buddhism very, how shall we say? – Enlightening.

The first: The world is swept away. It does not endure.

The second: The world is without shelter, without protector.

The third: The world is without ownership. One has to pass on, leaving everything behind.

The fourth: The world is insufficient, insatiable, a slave to craving.

When I read these, I was like, whoa! And the fourth item is what really clicked with me regarding my dilemma over multiple sexual partners.

When Ratthapala was asked what he meant when he said, "The world is insufficient, insatiable, a slave to craving," Ratthapala asked King Koravya: if he was informed of another rich country that he could conquer and add to his own kingdom, what would he do? The king replied he would attack and conquer that country. And if another? He would conquer that too. On and on and to what end?

So, for someone who believes it's OK to have multiple sexual partners as a regular lifestyle, someone comes up to you and says, "Hey, I know this hot dude who'd love to meet you." Would you want to meet him? And if so, what if someone else comes along and says, "Hey this hot dude wants to get with you?' Hey, why the heck not? And then maybe even this hot dude says, "Hey, I know this really hot guy who'd love a threesome." Are you gonna go for it?

It's all well and good except for one thing: you remain a slave to sensuality. You remain a slave to sensual indulgences. You think you're free, but in reality, you're not.

The other issue is the lack of intimacy in these relationships. I know someone who fits this, who told me he thinks he found someone he could "make a relationship with," although it was clear to me there was no love. It was a matter of convenience. And even after saying he was interested in this guy, he was still sleeping with other men.

But before you say I just endorsed monogamy over sleeping around, hold on. It's not that simple. And the person who posed the original question also included polyamory as an option. I'll get to that later.

The problem is not with sleeping around *per se*, but with human nature. We humans tend to be possessive. Remember? Greed, hatred, and delusion. Greed is first.

As my original questioner said, if everyone is on the same page about the arrangement, then all is well. But as soon as I or anyone else starts to cling to the relationship, denying that it will evolve and change, then we have a problem.

Does that make sleeping around inherently riskier than serial monogamy? Or even marriage?

Not really, because such interpersonal problems and issues of trust and intimacy are not just issues in nontraditional relationships. Trust and intimacy are often the prime issue behind why many monogamous relationships fail.

So you can see that it's not the structure of the relationship that makes it unskillful, but our own unskillful tendencies that can manifest themselves in any relationship structure. We all often talk about how important open communication is. But the fact remains, we're often not good at honest communication. And we're not good at it because of our greed, hatred, and delusion. We delude ourselves into thinking we're good communicators.

Which brings me to polyamory, which is not quite the same as an open relationship. In fact, I believe the structure of a polyamorous arrangement can be more stable and resilient than an open relationship.

Forgive me for taking the time to clarify these two arrangements. I have found that many intelligent and well-rounded people have significant misconceptions about both arrangements. And for that matter, there will be others to disagree with how I describe them. But for the purpose of this discussion, here it goes.

In an open relationship, there is a core couple. In general, this couple lives together and most of the sex involves the couple. The couple may or may not be married. That's irrelevant. The relevant factor is there's an agreement that either partner has permission from the other to seek other sexual encounters with other persons, either on their own or with the other partner (threesomes, for example).

Polyamory may or may not have a central couple. The key factor is that is everyone involved in the relationship knows about the other partners and may even know them on a personal level. And in my experience, the number of people involved in the relationship is limited to a degree. For example, I may love three different people, and I split my time between these three people, having sex at different times with each. I may spend a week with one, go on a vacation with another, have the third spend a month with me, etc. And each of them have multiple, but limited, "others" as well.

As a rule, there are no randoms in polyamory. Whereas in an open relationship, random hookups are allowed.

Perhaps falling within the rubric of polyamory is a situation in which there's a core couple who deeply love and care for one another, maybe even build a home together, but sex may not be very important to that couple. So one or both partners may cultivate another relationship that is mostly sexual.

I know such couples who love each other, but don't have sex often for various reasons. And one partner has some kinks they enjoy exploring, so he cultivates a relationship with someone just for that kink. Maybe he's a sub and cultivates a relationship with a dom outside of the main relationship.

Again, none of these relationships are inferior or superior to a traditional monogamous arrangement. Rather, it all falls back on what are your intentions when you act? Will your actions (thoughts, words, and deeds) lead to pleasant outcomes for you? For others? For you and others? Or will they lead to unpleasant outcomes for you? For others? For you and others?

And are you being honest when you assess the situation? Is everyone else being honest?

So it isn't the relationship structure that makes an arrangement more skillful than another, but how we act within that arrangement and how we relate with the others involved. Buddhism is an excellent tool for helping us navigate these and all our other personal relationships, including those we don't care much for at all.

And yet, Buddhism, like many other religions, has fallen into this rut of showing preference for some relationships over others, and even suggesting that being born homosexual is the result of one's kamma. That last bit, that being gay is the result of kamma, is really incredible because it's so reductionist: You are gay because of something negative you did in a previous life! Negative!

"Huh? I love being gay. If that's bad kamma, then bring me some more!"

Truth be told, the problem is not with Buddhism *per se*, but with some Buddhists. The teachings, throughout history, have been distorted in many ways to serve political agendas. In this respect, Buddhism is just as easily manipulated by self-serving teachers as how the words of Jesus get twisted by preachers and how Islam gets distorted by Imams.

Many a reader may believe that the issue of gay reparative therapy is a uniquely Western phenomena, but that would be inaccurate.

Within the past few decades, similar clinics have turned up in Malaysia. These clinics were for "sissy boys" and asserted they could turn your sissy boy into a real man. Unsurprisingly, many reparative therapists took up the torch – oh, how ironic – to practice this voodoo psychology in Malaysia where they found a willing client: The Malaysian government, which allegedly forced boys into the treatment centers. Despite international condemnation, the Malaysian government essentially replied with a hearty "fuck you."

But that's not the end of it. While it may not surprise you that conservative Christian groups and Islamic groups continue to support efforts to change one's sexuality, it may surprise you to learn that Buddhist organizations, teachers and even various Sanghas have been involved in reparative therapy as well.

There have even been news reports of a particular Thai Sangha's involvement in treating so-called "ladyboys."

To get a good grasp about how this issue operates in Thailand and most of Southeast Asia, one needs to understand both how the Sangha fits into Thai culture, as well as understand the history of the *kathoey*, or ladyboy, both in Thai culture and Buddhist history.

For this explanation, I'm going to rely heavily on a work by Peter A. Jackson called "Male Homosexuality and Transgenderism in the Thai Buddhist Tradition." Granted, this work dates back to 1993, but it nonetheless presents excellent background on this issue. (You can find it in the book *Queer Dharma: Voices of Gay Buddhists*, edited by Winston Leyland)

There remains a very strong link between the Sangha and lay community in SE Asia, where families in Thailand, Laos, Myanmar and Cambodia send their boys to the Sangha for short periods where they learn Dhamma and live as a novice monk.

Some decide to stay. Most return to their families and lay life.

This is such a strong tradition that surveys revealing that many Thais no longer support the Sangha like they had in the past made headlines in the local Thai press.

Many may have a perspective that Thais are generally very tolerant and accepting of homosexuality. After all, sex clubs have been ubiquitous in Bangkok and Pataya (not as much so in Phuket), and if you type the search terms "ladyboy" and "Thailand" into Google, you'll get a plethora of results for various websites offering a variety of services performed by such ladyboys.

True, there are no laws against homosexual activity in Thailand as there are in Malaysia to the south, but to conclude that homosexuality is widely accepted in Thailand would be very unskillful. It's not uncommon for Thai police to raid gay bars just for the hell of it, much like police did in the U.S. during the 1950s and 1960s.

What made the attitude different in Thailand from that in the West, Jackson points out, was the Thai attitude toward homosexuality was largely diffused: it lacked a specific target.

The AIDS epidemic in Thailand changed all that; it gave people who initially harbored vague feelings of antipathy toward homosexuals an opportunity to target them with aggressive hatred.

But where did this seed of homophobia come from?

Believe it or not, it came from several Thai Buddhist teachers from the past whose homophobic interpretations of the Tipitika have been carried forward by more recent members of the Thai Sangha.

As was largely the case with Christianity and Biblical texts, the Buddhist canon contains sections referring to certain, specific sexual activity and attitudes.

But given the fact there was no Western concept of homosexuality 2,500 years ago in Asia, modern Buddhist "interpreters" have tended to force the concept of homosexuality onto Pali terms and descriptions of activity that appear similar to what the Western mind labels as "homosexual."

Another thing to keep in mind is the Pali canon, and Thai Buddhism in particular, contains a very strong anti-sex message directed specifically toward monks.

"That which is called *methunadhamma* is explained as: the dhamma of an unrighteous man (*asattapurisa*), the conduct of the common people, the manners of the low, dhamma which is evil and crude, dhamma whose end is but water, an activity which should be hidden, the dhamma which couples should perform together." (*Vinaya*, Vol. 1, p. 49)

While the message was strident, it did not differentiate between forms. All types of sex were covered: it didn't matter what a monk stuck his penis into, such activity always carried the same result – the monk had failed and was usually expelled from the Sangha.

But a distaste for all forms of sex, even among the laity, found its way into the commentaries of many Thai Buddhist writers. Jackson writes:

"Significantly, contemporary Thai Buddhist views on laypersons' sexual behaviour are often more proscriptive and extreme than attitudes reflect in the Pali canon or in traditional or popular Thai accounts of Buddhist doctrine and ethics. Phra Buddhadasa's work has been especially influential among educated and middle class Thai Buddhists. However, his views on sexuality are at variance with Thai Buddhism's traditional distinction between lay and clerical ethical conduct. The ethical extremism of Phra Buddhadasa and other contemporary Buddhist reformists in Thailand such as Phra Phothirak results from a clericalizing trend **whereby ethical demands traditionally made only of monks are now increasingly also being required of laypersons**." (emphasis added)

This anti-sex attitude remains to this day, not only in the Thai Sangha but to a large extent within general Thai society among the laity in the form of homophobia.

The term *kathoey* in Thai loosely translates as "ladyboy" and has a somewhat interesting history in Buddhist literature. The term has been translated to include everything from hermaphrodites to being a descriptive term for a weakling or eunuch.

The Pali term *pandaka* has been used to describe virtually any sexual deviant, but was most frequently used to describe homosexual activity. Jackson writes:

> But whether or not Buddhism has been instrumental in influencing the development of the popular Thai notion, a very similar mixing

of physical and psychological sex, gender behaviours and sexuality occurs both in the Pali terms pandaka and in the Thai term kathoey. Both terms are parts of conceptual schemes in which people regarded as exhibiting physiological or culturally ascribed features of the opposite sex are categorised together. If Buddhism was not the source of the popular Thai conception of kathoey then at the very least it has reinforced a markedly similar pre-existing Thai cultural concept.

Jackson further states that the term kathoey has largely transformed in general Thai vernacular to be used to describe any gay man, whether a cross-dresser or straight-acting, so nowadays it essentially translates as "fag."

It is unfortunate that so many Thai commentators and their subsequent followers developed and promoted such anti-gay sentiments, as there are some very interesting references in the Pali canon to the Buddha showing great tolerance toward those whose sexual identity did not follow the norm.

There was Ananda, the Buddha's cousin and personal attendant, who allegedly was born a kathoey in many previous lives and who became an *arahant* (one who has gained insight into the true nature of existence and has achieved nibbana) shortly after the Buddha became enlightened.

And there is the story of Vakkali, who was enamored with the Buddha. The Buddha rebuked Vakkali for constantly staring lustfully at the Buddha, but his rebuke was not a "stop looking at me that way gay boy," but rather, stop falling into the trap of sensual attachment. Nonetheless, the Buddha told Vakkali to go away. Jackson writes:

> Vakkali was so shattered by this command that he attempted to kill himself by jumping off a mountain. But deva or spiritual beings informed the Buddha of Vakkali's dejection and he quickly went to the monk's aid in time to save him from committing suicide. With an extremely brief exposition of the dhamma, "The eyes see dhamma," the Buddha gave Vakkali the insight he needed in order to attain enlightenment and he immediately attained arahantship.

Even in the Buddha's time, homophobia was toxic. It created suicidal despair then as it does now.

Nonetheless, there is a proscription against ordaining a pandaka that is attributed to the Buddha based on a tale in the Vinaya about a monk who was running around the Sangha asking the young monks to "fuck me, fuck me."

When they didn't oblige, the pandaka went to the elephant stables and again pleaded with the men there to "fuck me, fuck me."

When the Buddha heard about this, he expelled the pandaka because he was concerned what the lay community might think about the Sangha. This has created considerable controversy today over whether openly gay men should be allowed to be ordained.

Now we're in the 21st Century when effeminate boys are being sent to Sanghas where monks are attempting to transform them from being pandaka or kathoey into real men, or *chai tae*. At work here is probably centuries of indoctrinated homophobia.

The renunciation of sexual desire, whether same-sex or opposite-sex, is for the monastic community and has everything to do with renouncing sensual pleasure of all types.

For the monks to teach these "ladyboys" to become "real men" would mean guiding these boys in the ways of hetero sex. The fact that monks would even venture into that territory at all with young novices strikes me as a serious corruption of Dhamma, as well as a particularly virulent form of homophobia sustained by reactionary abbots who don't know what to do with the ordained ladyboys in their midst.

And again we come back to the psychological trauma such reparative therapy can create in young minds.

This isn't the ending of suffering, this constitutes the nurturing and encouragement of suffering. Many of these boys will simply reject the efforts and return to their previous ways after they leave the Sangha.

But others may likely be so traumatized that they commit suicide or develop seriously self-destructive behaviors. From being happy, these boys are "transformed" into miserable waifs.

At the root of all this is misrepresenting duality, or binary thinking.

Duality in Buddhism is a common concept, one you can find references to regardless of vehicle – it's present in Theravada and Mahayana. It's also one of those Buddhist concepts that gets misused, is misunderstood, and can easily lead the unskilled into dangerous complacency.

I mean, seriously, I'm sorry that my eyes roll whenever I hear someone pontificate that, "Like, there's no wrong or right, you know? Those are just false concepts that are forced by a society that wants to, like, control you. You know?"

Gnarly, dude.

On the one hand, the idea that duality is a false concept in most of our experience is right on. Jim Wilson, in his essay for the second volume of *Queer Dharma*, provides a really nice explanation of duality and how it's a fabrication tenuously held together by a collective acceptance that it exists.

Wilson, in his essay "Practicing Buddhism As A Gay Man," uses the former "border" between East and West Germany to illustrate his point. For years, the world accepted the duality that there was an East Germany and a West Germany. Then one day, there was one Germany. Where did the line go? Was it even there except in our minds? For one period of time, the world agreed there were two Germanies, then one day, the world agreed there was one Germany.

Just like that.

Something a little more difficult for many to grasp is the notion of race and precisely how fluid it really is.

In her excellent 2014 article in *Salon*, "The History White People Need to Learn," Mary-Alice Daniel reveals that even the idea of "white people" hasn't always been clearly defined as a separate race.

In fact, it wasn't until people with white skin started to encounter with greater frequency people with skin other than white did "whites" perceive a need to collectively identify themselves as "white." Prior to that, races were divided according to nationalities (another fabrication, I know): For example, the Germans were a race different from the Italians, who were different from the Celts, and so on.

So, yes, race is a construct, a creation of mind. Having said that, there is a problem with being too ready to accept that as the way things are. Saying this is the way things are is not the same as seeing things as the way things are, and, frankly, I am skeptical when I hear Buddhists, in particular white Buddhists, say that.

It makes one lazy, providing an excuse to be unmotivated to tackle the real issues surrounding such "theoretical constructs" like race, gender, and sexuality in our sanghas.

Wilson's essay is exceptional for another reason beyond the way he describes the concept of dualism, and that is the role lesbigay practitioners play in disrupting the dualism surrounding gender identity.

> Because gay men, and other sexual minorities, do not fall within the categories of how the mind has structured male and female, the presence of gay men, simply by that presence, calls into question the dualistic consciousness upon which that division rests. I believe this goes a long way towards explaining why the presence of gay men provokes strong hostility from many people.

Just by showing up we completely disrupt long-held notions of not just sexuality, but gender roles – we turn them on their head! And just when some people think they've figured out the idea of gay and straight, we turn things upside down again with transgendered people, asexual people, and gender nonconforming.

It freaks people out, because some folks obsess themselves with why there's an apparent obsession over gender identification. The amazing thing is that this is nothing new, there have always been those who do not conform to the duality of male and female and the roles thereby assigned. Only now are people willing to say something about it and demand acceptance of their existence.

And even though race has always been somewhat fluid, it's become even more fluid as people are no longer accepting limited categorizations based on skin color. No, we are Hispanic black or Asian brown or Latino mulatto or whatever.

On one hand there are those who say, "stop all this nonsense! These are all just theoretical constructs!" But on the other hand, forcing the recognition of these differences pushes people out of their comfort zones, which had successfully insulated them from engaging other human beings as they are without first compartmentalizing them into easily recognized boxes of existence.

It can seem like alphabet soup out there when we talk about race, ethnicity, gender identity, or sexuality. And it's understandable that it can be frustrating. But so what? It becomes a problem only under two circumstances.

One is when others push back against this process of self-identification. The reason for pushing back is defensive and selfish because these "new" labels disrupt and challenge previously-held sacred beliefs about who and what people are.

Such self-identification also challenges the power structure that remains largely under the control of straight white males, both in and out of the various Buddhist communities.

The second circumstance is when people present a facade that they are beyond prejudice and privilege by retreating to the position that these are all fabrications that we just need to relinquish.

But such a position is not letting go; the fabrication is, in fact, retained and strengthened into an even more-secure delusion.

And besides, our Buddhist precepts demand that we journey beyond this.

The Fourth Precept encourages us to refrain from lying. Ignoring our personal identities would be a violation of the precept. As every one of us now out of the closet knows, denying our sexual identity is to relegate ourselves to a personal hell. Coming out is freedom, it's liberation, and Buddhism is all about liberation.

So yeah, we're here, we're queer, and we're here to help you.

About the Author

My first encounter with Buddhism was in 1999, to the best of my recollection. I was dating a Thai man at the time who invited me to go with him to a celebration of the Buddha's birth, enlightenment, and death, known as Visakha Puja (usually in May during the full moon). More commonly this day is called Buddha Day.

At the time I was living in Mount Pleasant, Michigan, as was the Thai man I was dating. He was a graduate student at Central Michigan University there, and I a newspaper reporter and editor. The Buddha Day celebration was in a rural community, Perry, Michigan, near the state capital, Lansing. It was about a ninety-minute drive.

I was intrigued by the invitation and thought, why not? I was raised Roman Catholic, but had abandoned the church long before, as well as even the remotest belief in a creator god. I remain spiritually inquisitive, however. I had dabbled with Native American spirituality for quite some time, but eventually lost interest in that as well because it still relied on interventions by a higher power. The Tao had a stronger hold on me because despite the Tao being a sort of higher power, it was not an "intelligent" one, as in a conscious entity.

Upon arrival I was quickly immersed in Thai culture. I humbly accepted tasks to set up a noon food banquet, as well as setting up chairs in a hall near the main house for an event scheduled for later. The food was marvelous, the smell of spice filled the air like a drug. Before anyone ate, however, a bowl with a helping from every dish – and there were dozens – was prepared and then taken to the abbot of this interesting place. Then we were allowed to eat and socialize.

After cleaning up, we departed for the rest of the afternoon until the evening activities. This was when I first saw the abbot, a white man, which I must say rather surprised me. I was quickly guided in proper etiquette prior to taking part in a ritual that had us circumnavigating a tree while holding a candle and three incense sticks. After rounding the tree three times, I followed everyone's lead and made a proper prostration before a Buddha statue where I placed my candle and incense sticks.

The entire procession both struck me as odd and soothing, odd because it just seemed like a lot of ritual and came very close to appearing like the Buddha was being worshiped as a god, soothing because the repetitive chanting involved, along with the walking in circles, made me feel tranquil and at ease.

After leaving our candles and incense before the Buddha statue that was hauled outside earlier, we all gathered in the nearby hall where the abbot gave a "Dhamma talk," much like a sermon or homily. He talked about the Five Precepts, explained them quite simply, and when he discussed the Third Precept, he went out of his way to explain that it didn't matter whether someone was gay or straight. The mechanics of sex weren't important; it was how you treated others.

That resonated with me. It was the first time in my experience I felt included. He also explained that we don't worship the Buddha as a god, but rather all this ritual was part of building concentration and stillness within the mind. Same with the chanting, it was not "praying," but something that helped calm the mind.

"There is nothing to pray for because there is nothing to pray to," he said. "The Buddha is gone. We are merely paying our respect and showing thanks for the Dhamma that he brought us."

The following weekend, the Dhammasala, or monastery where the monk resided, was moving. My Thai boyfriend recruited me to come help with the move, which was fine with me. The old location was on a small suburban plot of land, probably no more than two acres in size. The new location, apparently donated by a couple of retired hippies, was twenty acres of rural, mostly wooded property.

Again, I was treated to a feast of delicious, homemade Thai dishes. I remember sitting on a grassy slope by the main house at the new location, feeling such peace and tranquility. I also briefly chatted with the abbot and learned he was from Midland, Michigan, the same town I was born in. It seemed he may have attended Midland High School at the same time as my brother, but he said he didn't recall many people from those days. After graduating, he ran away to become a Buddhist monk.

Shortly after that weekend when we moved the Dhammasala to its new location, I broke up with my boyfriend. And that was my last contact with the monastery for a while. I eventually began dating someone else, which developed into a very intense affair. But this was before marriage equality, and my new boyfriend was a Chinese man from Indonesia. He was also a graduate student at the time, and after finishing his masters degree, his student visa would run out and he'd have to leave unless he found a job.

We were madly in love. The thought of him leaving, of having to return to Indonesia, was unbearable. But it could not be avoided. After his plane departed and I returned home, I sat on the toilet and wailed, cried so hard I was convulsing. It truly felt as though there was a hole in my chest.

And the pain lingered. Work didn't provide any salve. Work did give me something to do, because outside of work, I did very little.

Then one day the thought occurred to me, "What if I go visit that monk?" Out of the blue the idea came to me. And right at that moment, I got into my car and drove the ninety minutes to the monastery. I had no idea what I was going to do once I got there. All I knew was that I felt a strong need to be there.

Because I had helped with the move, I remembered how to get there. When I arrived, I saw the monk standing with some others by a partially built gazebo in a meadow about two hundred yards away. I walked toward them. As I approached, the monk looked at me, then spoke to the others. They also looked at me. As I got nearer, the monk began to walk away from them back toward the main house. As he neared me, I made a slight bow, then told him my name, that I had been there before, I had helped with the move.

"Yes, I know who you are," the monk replied as he kept walking past me.

A bit flummoxed, I stood there uncertain what to do next. It was then one of the men by the gazebo called to me.

"Do you know how to use a hammer?"

I nodded, then took a few steps toward them. Within minutes, I was helping them build the gazebo.

That began a routine of weekly visits to the Dhammasala where I participated in Dhamma lessons, meditation sessions, and helped finish the gazebo. I also helped rebuild a collapsed porch attached to the main house, and construct a new meditation hall.

I had become Buddhist. My world was restored.

When I moved from Mount Pleasant to Holland, Michigan, I was further away from the Dhammasala – it's known as Wat Dhammasala and Monastery – and couldn't go every weekend. But I made the effort to go for special events. And by the time I had moved to Chicago, my knowledge and experience with Buddhism was at a level I could sustain a practice on my own. That was when I began the blog, *My Buddha is Pink*.

This book is one more step along the path. I have much further yet to go.

☸

www.ingramcontent.com/pod-product-compliance
Lightning Source LLC
Chambersburg PA
CBHW030141170426
43199CB00008B/162